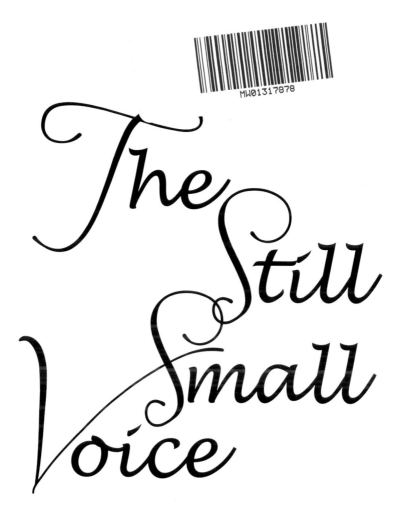

Stephanie M. Lumbia

The Still Small Voice

© 2013 Stephanie M. Lumbia

All Rights Reserved. No part of this publication may be produced or transmitted in any form or by any means without written permission of the author. The author guarantees all contents are original and do not infringe upon the legal rights of any other person or work.

Editor's Note: The author has a unique writing style that communicates her speaking to God, listening to His voice, and hearing things in her spirit. Sometimes her journal entries of these impressions breaks common rules of punctuation. In an effort to preserve the writer's style and remain true to her original manuscript and intent, these areas have been left alone—as she wants them to appear.

Printed in the U.S.A.
ISBN: 978-0-9857942-9-3

Scripture quotations taken from the Amplified® Bible, Copyright © 1954, 1958, 1962, 1964, 1965, 1987 by The Lockman Foundation. La Habra, CA. Used by permission.

Scripture taken from the King James Version of the Bible ®, Copyright © 1982 by Broadman & Holman Publishers, Nashville, TN. Used by permission. All rights reserved.

Scripture taken from The Message ®. Copyright © 1993, 1994, 1995, 1996, 2000, 2001, 2002. Used by permission of NavPress Publishing Group. Colorado Springs, CO. All rights reserved.

Scripture taken from the HOLY BIBLE, NEW INTERNATIONAL VERSION ®. Copyright © 1973, 1978, 1984 Biblica. Used by permission of Zondervan. All rights reserved.

Scripture taken from the New King James Version (NKJV) of the Bible. Copyright © 1982 by Thomas Nelson, Inc. Used by permission. All rights reserved.

Scripture quotations are taken from the Holy Bible, New Living Translation, copyright 1996, 2004. Used by permission of Tyndale House Publishers, Inc., Wheaton, Illinois 60189. All rights reserved.

To Contact the Author for speaking engagements:
visit: *www.stephaniemlumbia.com*
email: *stephaniemlumbia@gmail.com*

Dedication

I Love Carrousels, but I Would Rather Take a Train

Yes I said, "Hmmm …" too! This book is dedicated to all who have taken the same route more often than they would like to, ending with the same results every time. The carrousel may change, but the lead horse reflecting in the mirror always looks the same. Sooner or later we get tired of being on the same ride—the same routine leading nowhere. We try to slow it down, change the scenery, and move to another ride, only to find it too is tirelessly familiar, and we shrink down in defeat. We ask, "How did I get here? We exclaim, "Not again!" Without recognizing that we are making a habitual choice, we get right back on the same ride, traveling in circles instead of moving forward.

How do we get off this carrousel? How do we break the habit and never return to the same routine of self-destruction?

If these two topics "Carrousels" and "Trains" look completely different, it's because they are! As I began to seek the Lord for truth, He put me on the fast track—the straight and narrow path, traveling with an exponential rate of speed into the realm of my predetermined destiny. How grateful I am to be forever changing, forever growing younger. I am His child … and His favorite one!

This book is dedicated to imparting blessings on all who have come to know Christ and also the ones who are yet to know Christ.

To my loving Father, whose love conquerors all. He endearingly nourished me when I was hungry and placed my feet upon solid rock. To the One who gave His life for mine, Jesus, I am forever rejoicing with all of heaven!

To my husband, who always loves me and stands with me. You enter the dream with me, till completion … and then some. I am truly blessed by your committed heart that encases mine. I love you with all that I am!

To my mother and father who loved me with the Lord's agape heart.

To Anne Grace, I have read so many books since that first book class with you. Too many to number! I used to read and

The Still Small Voice

write stories in my youth frequently, but put that on the shelf for the past 25 years. You came into my life and brought me into my future, writing. Thank you for an obedient heart in which you opened the door for a writing club. You made it inviting even for a beginner, like me. The Lord told me I would write a book when I moved here. In His grace, and in His perfect timing, I wrote my first story. Thank you dearly for expediting this journey for me. You will always be dear to my heart.

To my dearest Patrice Wallace, who always celebrated my steps. I'm so grateful the Lord has chosen you as my friend whom I can share this life with. Your feedback encourages me to be more real in my writing, and to openly share the depths of my heart. For the endearing and passionate heart of love you have for my husband and me, may God bless you beyond measure. We love you with all that we are.

To my friends who touched my heart with their truest hearts after God.

To all who allowed me to fall down, but get back up again,

B-L-E-S-S-I-N-G-S!

Leave the carrousel behind.
Hop aboard the train,
He is waiting for you!

Nothing can separate us from the Father.

The Still Small Voice

"Being confident of this, that He who began a good work in you,

Will carry it on to completion until the day of Christ Jesus."

—Philippians 1:6 NIV

Contents

	Introduction	11
1.	*Released Within Me*	13
2.	*Lord, Don't Pass Me By*	17
3.	*Heavenly Feathers*	23
4.	*No, Just Yours*	25
5.	*Portion*	27
6.	*A New Creature in Christ*	29
7.	*The Crowned One*	35
8.	*Promise Land*	37
9.	*Scepter of Righteousness*	41
10.	*Miracle Healing*	43
11.	*No Longer Lukewarm*	49

The Still Small Voice

12.	Rose of Sharon	53
13.	When Something Ends	55
14.	Crown Upon My Head	59
15.	Dying of Self	63
16.	The Lord is On My Treadmill	67
17.	I Need You	69
18.	Clear Access	73
19.	No Distractions	75
20.	Strawberry Fields	79
21.	Come Walk With Me	83
22.	Wisdom in a Breakthrough	85
23.	Lack of Knowledge	89
24.	My Father's Daughter	93
25.	Loving Patience	95
26.	Fishes and Loaves	99

The Still Small Voice

27.	When Did I Enlist?	103
28.	Lion's Den	105
29.	Believe	111
30.	If God Be For Us	115
31.	I Am the Fruit	121
32.	Lobster on My Plate	125
33.	The Gem of the Sea	129
34.	Just Follow Me	133
35.	He Reigns	139
36.	His Courts	143
37.	Gotcha'	147
38.	Keys to the Kingdom	153
39.	Mirror, Mirror on the Wall	155
40.	Stop, Sit, and Pray	159
41.	A Fresh Revelation	163

42.	His Name Above All Names	167
43.	The Holy of Holies	169
44.	The Master Groomer	173
45.	Beautiful	181
46.	Overcomer	185
47.	Jeremiah 29:11	191
48.	Provision	195
49.	Inheritance	199
50.	The Wilderness	201
51.	Be Prepared	205
52.	It's in the Small Things	211

Introduction

This book was written with purposeful intent to reveal how love can transform from the inside out. It is presented to you as my journal entries, in chronological order as I wrote them. You will be able to see the progression of my transformation as the journal entries get deeper and more confident. Often as I wrote, I would hear as He communicated with me, often taking over my pen!

As you begin reading, it is important that you know there was a time when I believed my own agenda was sufficient in all ways ... until one day, God reached down for me. He chose me to be an Ambassador of Christ! From that moment forth, I wanted to be filled with the Spirit of God in every area of my life.

In *The Still Small Voice*, I open my heart to the reader and share candidly about the intimate transformation that cost me everything. My true life story demonstrates the rewards a life in Christ has to offer—freedom! The genuine, sacrificial love that overcame everything, has now has taken territory and conquered every corner of my life. I willingly relinquished myself to the Great I AM.

His promises conquered victoriously over my broken life, as I trusted, taking one step at a time. Until I experienced that Jesus' love never fails, I was never really truly alive. This book is about leaving self-righteousness behind and becoming the righteousness of God in Christ.

Compared to eternity, this journey on earth is temporal and just a blink. My deepest heartfelt desire is to behold the fullness of God's great love and then give it all away freely.

I share my triumphs and failures with men and women of all ages. I share it particularly for those who are seeking to achieve permanent results in their own lives. He holds our true identity and this becomes authentic as we walk into the truth of God. I am forever changing through the relentless pursuit of Jesus, abiding in His love—desiring nothing more than Him and accepting nothing less.

My transformation was possible only by the power of the Holy Spirit. He and He alone restored my heart, renewed my mind, and renovated my soul. It was by Him. It was through His redemptive, precious blood, that I was saved from myself. I remember saying, "One day, I would like to stop writing the story and become the story." That is exactly what happened!

As you read this book, I invite you to experience your own conversations with God, to behold the all the treasures of His wonders and loving grace that surpass all understanding. Come walk with me and drink from the cup of the Everlasting.

Stephanie

One

Released Within Me

The Lord led me go to my extended secret place to pray—my bedroom! As I pressed in to hear the Lord's voice, I opened my heart to know **"His will for me and plan for my life ..."** As I journaled His precious words to me, He finished my sentence with, **"... would be released."** The words were clearly His, not mine.

On January 8, 2010 while on day six of my very first fast, God had already given me my assignment. This morning's prayer caused the true **release of it!** I kept a journal during my fast. I wrote, "Fasting is a form of worship that will humble you. Remind yourself of your dependency on God." On the next line I wrote, "I can do nothing apart from God. I need Him like I need the air to breathe. Harmoniously, I breathe in and He exhales."

The next section of my journal was my prayer focus for the day. Although I didn't read it until after dinner, I anxiously picked up my book, *Fasting* by Jentzen Franklin.

It said, "God has given you gifts to use for His purpose. Pray and meditate and seek God about His purpose and plan for your life, your ministry unto Him." With this directive I prayed and this is what I heard:

"Ministry ... worship ... speak"

I was hungry for more. I wanted to hear Him clearly. Even though I knew I was with Him all day, I craved for more of Him. I ran into my bedroom to pay closer attention to His voice in the quiet stillness. I prayed to be where He was—not for Him to come to where I was. When He immediately took me to a spiritual place, I began a heartfelt prayer. "Lord, I want to know your truth." He spoke back to me:

"Deny Yourself"

I breathed in slowly and let His words sink deep inside of me. I waited in silence, expectant. Then He clearly said, **"Give it up."** Not comprehending, I asked, "Give what up, Lord?"

"You," He said. **"All. Now."**

I knelt on the floor, pleading with the Lord in deep passion and love for Him. I cried so deeply. I wailed with an aching heart. I shuddered at His desire for me. When He spoke to me I saw Him on a cross with deep, deep blue behind Him. It was so heart-wrenching. It was as if someone had taken a sword to my heart. This reached a place so deep inside my heart that it could only have been the place where I could really meet Him. I was humbled before Him. He was so clearly present there with me, I bowed my knee. It was compelling and real. I continued praying for His truth regarding my life. I inquired after His plan for me, in depth.

All I could do was cry from the core of genuine truth. I know He had me pray out His spirit. From this place I released the innermost part of my heart. I was naked before the Lord. He saw my original ordained days. He saw the authentic rawness of my desire, and He saw that it was for Him.

He spoke gently to me, **"Get up now"**.

I did. I draped over my bed, utterly spent and said, "I want to serve you Lord."

"Show me your heart," He said.

I cried as He took me to the root of things in my heart. I repented of formal sins I had not let go. I lifted everything to Him. He requested that I be verbally specific, and so I was.

The next thing I knew, I was before Him and appeared as if I was kneeling. I saw the hem of His garment and His feet with sandals. His garment was a very deep blue. I realized I was like the woman in the Bible ... who just wanted to touch the hem of His garment, so desperately. As I spiritually climbed over the obstacles to reach Him, I was not going to let this opportunity quaintly fall side. I was too desperate for Him! With outstretched arms, I projected my fingers to cling to His robe. I wanted Jesus more than I wanted my own life.

"Lord," I said, "Use me as Your servant to love the people. Save them unto You." I cried profusely, burdened for the lost." There are so many who don't know You. They need ... You. They belong to You, not to this world." I longed to be used by Him. "Oh Lord, please, *please* use me."

"All of your days?" He asked.

I replied sincerely, with tears streaming down my cheeks and said, **"<u>All</u> of my days."**

So as I sit and recount this anointed time with Jesus, He spoke to me once again and said ... He had released Himself within me.

Oh Lord, how I love Thee,

Stephanie

"As the deer pants for streams of water,
so my soul pants for You, my God."

—Psalm 42:1 NIV

Two

Lord, Don't Pass Me By

I thought if I ate less, or changed what food I was consuming for my fast It could result in showing more dedication to God. So, I asked my friend Jesus, "What do You want me to eat? Vegetables and water only?"

He replied so gently, "Stephanie, it's not what you eat, it's what you give."

My eyes were filled with tears as my heart became full ... it was filled with His compassionate level of love! I acknowledged,

"He wants all of me!"

Tonight at church, I saw the same vision that I saw on Sunday, but added to the vision was also me desperately reaching to touch the hem of His garment. I saw His feet and robe again! I was crawling, stretching, desperately reaching out to touch Him—be with Him, love Him, adore Him, needing Him beyond anything else. I couldn't be satisfied with just a little as I gasped to touch Him. My heart felt the

desire of wanting so much more. Nothing was going to hold me back!

The crowd parted slightly as a narrow passageway allowed my arm to reach in. "It's me Lord, it's me," I cried on the inside. My frantic heart ached to know Him more. It didn't matter how I looked, just as long as I got there. I was unrelenting in my pursuit until I reached Him. Whatever cost or measure it took, anything that barricaded me from reaching Him, I would break through. All for the sake of love ... to bond with Him. Like the woman in Mark I thought as she did:

> *"If I just touch his clothes, I will be healed."*
> *All at once Jesus realized that power had gone out from Him. He turned around in the crowd and asked, "Who touched my clothes?"*
> *"You see the people crowding against you," his disciple answered, "and yet you can ask, "Who touched me?"*
>
> *Mark 5:28* NIV

I shared what I saw with a small group of friends afterwards. I won't forget their faces! One saw our hands open and a dove landing in one!

He continued sharaing with me as I worshipped in rich immersion ...

I saw a village set in biblical times. There were buildings on the right with walls that looked like they were covered in stucco and tall buildings on the other side. It looked like a town. It was colorful and I knew I was in the presence of the Lord prior to the vision, but, here He came with a large procession of people behind Him. Some (apparently leaders) were in front of Him. I saw Him in a red robe. Then it looked as if He was riding a donkey! As He proceeded near me, I yelled out to Him, waving my hands. I was on the second or third floor of a building, leaning out an open window frame. I was leaning out and shouting:

> "Here I am, Lord help me! Lord give me,
> and Lord fill me, Lord Look at me!"

It was all about me getting His attention. I wasn't going to let this opportunity pass me by, at any cost.

But as quickly as I spoke, I saw a pipeline come to me, convicting me instantly. Once I realized that I needed to seek Him I began shouting,

> "I need You Lord, I glorify You, Your majesty, Your
> forgiveness, oh precious Lord, King of Kings!"

The Holy Spirit showed me it wasn't all me—it wasn't "give me, give me, give me." It was praising, worshipping, giving thanks, and seeking Him. He then looked up at me acknowledging me with a smile as everything else in the picture grew dim and quiet. Our eyes met, our hearts became one. It was as if no one else was there. Something profound happened. An exchange occurred and I was brought into a personal relationship with Him.

I was convicted:

**"Are you going to let Him pass you by?
Are you going to miss Him?"**

The church body will miss Him, He will pass them by. You don't know when and even if He'll pass by here again. I desperately reached out for Him. We all need to. But the beautiful and heartfelt part about all this was that He never went ahead of me! He stopped and received me and never took another step forward! He never passed me! Then the vision was over. I know I was with Him at that very moment and it was real.

I have had this encounter twice now and He gave me this awesome opportunity to participate freely. I hunger for Him, I claw for Him, and I love Him so much.

Tonight at Supernatural School of Ministry classes, we began to watch a video, and the Holy Spirit began to minister to me. I wrote what I heard:

"Don't be busy with things to do when you have Me to assign you. I will instruct you, the Almighty, for the sake of the kingdom of God. Seek Me first, I will command you. Until then, listen with intent upon the things which I will appoint you to. Always."

Then He added ... "Like Jesus."

After watching the video I asked the Lord, "Which mountain are we taking?" I reminded God that were not ready yet and He spoke to me, "Almost there."

The Still Small Voice

What a full day in the Lord!

"Lord,

"How I thirst for You. I will seek You for the rest of my life. You are so precious and You didn't pass me by. Amen."

Hungry and thirsting for You,

Stephanie

The Still Small Voice

"*If you abide in Me, and My words abide in you, you will ask what you desire, and it shall be done for you. By this My Father is glorified, that you bear much fruit; so you will be My disciples.*"

—John 15:7-8 NKJV

Three

Heavenly Feathers

It was as if someone took my head and turned it purposefully, placing my eyes upon a feather on my kitchen floor today. I would never have seen it without God pointing it out, it was camouflaged by the pale colors of my tile. Another appeared under my kitchen dinette chair. But just as soon as I saw them ... they disappeared ... out of sight!

"What is going on?" I thought. "Are these real," I wondered, " ... or by coincidence?" As I sang in worship and abided in His presence all day at home, music filled the air and my heart sang out.

Could this have been a sign of angels present?

When my husband arrived home from work, I shared my first time gifts with him in peaceful glory. I was completely overcome with joy at the possibility of existing angels in our home! Then I explained another sighting with him as he stood in the doorway of our bedroom.

As I stood alongside my bed, a feather was standing up in my bedspread, in front of me, in plain sight. I picked it up and questioned its validity. Then I asked the Lord, "Please don't put feathers in my bedroom, because I'll forever question them. I will wonder if they are from my pillows and not from angels."

So, I said to my husband, my back to the window, facing him across the room, in the place of evidence, "Can you believe it? Do you think it is real?"

He looked at me, smiled and said, **"I don't know about that, but the one floating over your head sure is!"**

Stunned, I quickly looked above my head and watched it gently fall, trying to capture it. It faded out of sight. I searched the floor. Nothing. It disappeared!

"Wow, God, you sent us a visible wonder!"

Convinced,

Stephanie

Four

No, Just Yours

While landscaping at my favorite place today, my mind was just spinning with thoughts. So, I stopped it and decided to have a two way conversation with God, instead of just one-sided, just talking about me all the time!

So, I began …

"Lord, how's Your day going? You've got a lot to deal with. With all these people, and compounded by all their problems and concerns …"

"No," He said, "Just Yours!"

Laughing with You!

Stephanie

The Still Small Voice

"A merry heart doeth good
like a medicine ..."
—Proverbs 17:22a KJV

Five

Portion

I woke this morning, and before I even got out of my bed, I was compelled to pray. I welcomed the Holy Spirit with arms wide open. I said I would abide in Him. Then I said, "You're my ..." and God spoke, "... portion."

I paused for just a moment, then heard again in my spirit, "You're my portion." How beautiful! It is the first time I have ever heard this! I just stopped and drank it in. Jesus revealed the Israelites in the desert and how He fed and took care of them—one day at a time—with no need to be concerned about tomorrow. This was an understanding I desperately needed to acquire myself. He is sufficient in all things. He supplies all my needs. He feeds me upon the word and I drink of Him. He is more than enough. He gives me my daily portion.

Day by day!

"Thank you, Lord. I love you so dearly. I have come into the truth as You transcend my heart. Amen"

Filled and satisfied with You,

The Still Small Voice

"You are my portion, Lord.
I have promised
to obey Your words."

—Psalms 119:57 NIV

Six

A New Creature in Christ

Today I moved very slowly, pondering my marriage relationship. My husband went to the men's breakfast at church. I was surprised that he was excited about going. Much to his surprise and mine, he truly had a God-encounter while there. When he returned, his face beamed from his experience of fellowship, participation, etc. So, I wrote this to my dear friend. A humbling confession:

> We were right about my husband. He really is growing by leaps and bounds! I have been a little confused and concerned about our relationship, because now it is taking a turn for the better. The enemy wants to scare me and make me feel weak, but my God is showing me what He is doing in us. We are both becoming stronger in the Lord—together—equipped to do His will. My beloved husband is taking leadership, not just in our relationship, but in the world also! This is good. But, I kind of miss my needy friend. (I'm just being honest.) I

know it's going to be all God-abounding and turn out superb, but it kind of leaves me feeling a bit scared sometimes. Truth was; I was out of control. Do you have any input on this?

My friend responded with encouragement and sent gobs of love my way. She reminded me that God knows all the details of my life and cares about them. He will answer me.

AND HE DOES!

In an "elevated discussion," I brought it to my husband's attention that his old behavior was not acceptable. I let him know that I didn't want that anymore. Yet, though I didn't want it, I seemed to focus on it and become angry about it. I wanted it to go away: the jealousy, accusations, rejection … oh, yuck! Wondering why I had this flip of emotions when I was filled with the peacefulness of worship and was totally calm.

Then, my great, wonderful Lord gave me this huge revelation, … after we have our foolish squabble, of course.

God showed me a vision. It was of me and a man with a suit on, a brief case in his hand, and dark hair. I saw his profile standing over to the right, and I jump with excitement and said, "That's who I want … a business man … a business man … he knows how to love me!"

This vision was a re-visitation of the man I first saw when I first met the man I now call my husband! Within his heart

was the love I knew was for me as he *"GQ'd"* across the walkway that ignited my palpitating heart! I saw him in a certain light while courting that peeked into his future. I call this ... destiny!

In contrast to the vision, today I didn't see that business man in his suit, capturing my heart. Today I saw all of my husband's old nature instead. This made me angry, because I didn't want that here. I sincerely desired what my heart cried out for ... Genuine Godly love. I had kept quiet for some time, then today I leaped out and told my husband all about his faults. Yes, I did that!

(As I journal about this, I am surprised that I did this, knowing very well I have enough faults of my own! It is much easier to point out someone else's sins, than it is to see your own. The Lord will use others to polish you up!)

I was shown a picture of ... well, of all my husband's old nature. Troubled I asked, "Why is this pointed out to me?"

Then the Lord said, "Be careful, are you calling this in?"

When the Lord spoke, my spirit gave me understanding. I asked myself, "Is this so familiar to you that you want this behavior?" Whoa! That was a shocking awakening!

I really took time to process this one. Living waters had been activated! I had to look at my behavioral patterns and seek understanding with this. I had to choose between an old pattern or seeking the Lord to reveal truth and uproot the lies. Oh, how I pray for a clean heart.

What had become comforting and familiar wasn't what the Lord had in mind. What I found security in was destroying me … and my new marriage. It was like a self-destructive, agreeable virus. One I needed deliverance from. To have the comfort of genuine love bestowed upon me and to give it away is my true heart's desire. I don't want to operate in destruction or out of self-preservation. But it is difficult to be vulnerable enough to allow the true flow of love to abide in me. I truly want a wholesome, Godly relationship. So, I have turned myself in an awakening through conviction from Christ today. My Lord heals!

The teaching which came by revelation will forever change me. Though I never meant to, I had been holding my husband in contempt, because of what was holding me. Although I didn't want the characteristics of darkness, they were familiar and assured. I was well acquainted with them … they had almost become my "bff"! They replaced the truth with a lie—a lie we were not even aware we were cooperating with. It fed my insecurity. What I truly desired in my heart was the genuine love God implanted. I had substituted many counterfeits for the true love I craved. See, we are made for love, but our ways of getting it aren't always the right choices.

I needed to unlearn what was retaining me from the real living breath of God Himself who holds all of life's gifts.

So, I made a choice. I chose to focus on God's blessings and call it as if it's already done, in both of us. Today I had to look into the mirror and take the plank out of my eye instead of trying to remove the splinter from my husband's eye. God's revelation took me to the roots of the problem and I am pulling them out. No longer will I be held in bondage.

We are to call out the King and the Priest in one another. When we focus on the sin, we make it big. But when we focus instead on Jesus in the person, we make Christ huge! It squashes out the enemy, swallows the sin, and truly brings forth a new creature.

So many relationships start out good, but turn as we fall into our old behaviors that aren't appealing or beneficial. If we can learn to be honest within ourselves and leave the bitterness behind long enough for God to do a good work in us, we will never be the same again! There is only better!

Today ... the chains fell off! And who the Son sets free, is free indeed!

What I did today was personally release my dear husband of his old nature and oppression (as well as mine), and allow him to move forth into his destiny. It is truly a new day. How blessed I am! For it is not what he is doing, but what I was believing. A permanent shift had taken a turn today.

I have repented (turned away) from judgment of him and myself. The King has decreed us to live in freedom. The Judge has rendered the sentence: "Not Guilty!"

To characterize myself or accuse anyone else of less than God's best, is not in anyone's best interest. Here is a word to the wise: take a look at yourself ... then pray, pray a lot!

The Still Small Voice

"Do not (earnestly) remember the former things; neither consider the things of old."

Isaiah 43:18 AMP

"Lord, I love my husband dearly. Please forgive me for holding him back in any way."

"Forgive me. I am sorry for holding you captive to your old nature in my mind. I love you with all my heart and will live out all my days on the earth beside you, Leonardo. I respect you."

With the highest love, honor, and respect,

Stephanie

Note to the Reader: *I was hesitant to share this story. I did not want to harm anyone. But if this example allows freedom to overcome someone else's bondage in this same area, I'm willing to take the risk. Oh, how Jesus comes gently to His Bride to relinquish her! Amen.*

Seven

The Crowned One

I just finished reading *The Supernatural Ways of Royalty* by Kris Vallotton and Bill Johnson. The following was inspired by insights from the book.

The eruption of the sound of Jubilee unleashed through all the nations will be the ultimate crowd pleasing victory!

Who will be the one? Who wants to be the one? Who will be chosen?

There is an inheritance wrapped in velvet and gold, in thorns and lashes. Not sought after, it would be like a gift never opened. Left, returned to sender. Or perhaps it will be weathered and broken, over time as our generations fail to recognize the Crowned One. I heard Him say, "Will there be one among you who will seek after Me and join with me to exalt thy King?"

He continued, "Would you lift the curtain and proceed with diligence and curiosity? Does there exist a true burning

desire that beckons your heart to extend yourself into the realm of the unseen? Do you deeply desire truth? For I would not leave you. I would not leave all that I have died for to be like dust in the wind. I would not leave you uncovered and exposed. My precious treasures are for those who know Me and call Me Father. For I have laid them beyond the cross. I have hidden them just for you.

"I call you My family ... whom I love, upon which I sacrificed Myself on the cross so you could be Mine. I have wrapped you in the riches of royalty and love. I have bestowed on you all the gifts from My Father above."

"You will be given a new name that I have laid upon your head. This name will direct you into which I have called and upon which I will strengthen you with the Holy One and promise to never leave you or forsake you.

"For you are my chosen one, the one I adore and love. I will give you the inheritance, will you give me yours?"

Crowned,
Stephanie

Eight

Promise Land

Where I am positioned? I need to know. I have felt completely lost from last Friday through this Wednesday morning. A fierce new battle began! In response, I released God and heaven over me, and claimed back the territory that the accuser stole.

He has tried so hard to take it back. Sneaky accuser! I received clarity last Wednesday afternoon. I had been experiencing a sense of confusion and heaviness, along with the entire weaponry unleashed by the enemy. I am being attacked with heavy artillery! I acknowledged that I was under fire. I tried to reason with understanding and by praying and releasing God in my life, but I felt like I was drowning. "How do I defeat it?" I wondered. It was overwhelming. I didn't know how to overcome this onslaught.

Then I was given a vision of a sword in my hand! This was how God revealed to me that I was going to win the battle!

He placed the sword in my hand. This was the first time I ever saw this. Wow!

So, as the day went on, the confusion lifted and my clarity returned. I received righteousness, with the Lord's grace and protection. I put on a mighty warrior's battle gear.

We went to Bible study that evening and the pastor preached about all that was going on with me for the past week.

Outside, in the parking lot, I shared my trials with my friend, Jacquelina. She smiled and said, "You killed some big giants this week!"

Stunned, I chuckled, and was immediately shown this vision. God took my eyes to the tall pine trees in the parking lot. There was a maze between them, intertwining through them. I was caught weaving between the giants in the thick, tall, dark forest. I could only look up to see the solution. I cried out, "Lord, help me!" And He delivered me out!

I then realized where I was. He had taken me out of the quiet place with Him—the place where I have been basking in the perfume of His love for two years! It was a beautiful time of just being washed and coming to know the Father personally. I just experienced His truth. I saw myself on the edge a few months ago, where the land met the water. Then, into the water I went! I went a little deeper each time. I knew I had entered into the same water that Peter walked on. (I consider this the trust test!)

What happened this week is this: I came to the other side! I came to a place where I had been praying diligently and intently during the past two months. I have been waiting patiently to live the life God has called me to since birth. Well, when I stepped onto the land ... I was met with the evil giants who stood in opposition to me entering. But I say with confidence, I won! The victory is mine. I am taking territory!

My inheritance will be washed upon the faith that Jesus died for me. (I heard this in my spirit.)

I am in the Promised Land! Wow!

Lord,

"May you always have access to my heart and ways. I commit all I am to You to fulfill the commission set ahead of me. I am Yours. Guide me and protect me as I journey into this new land."

Amen

Thankful,

Stephanie

The Still Small Voice

"For the weapons of our warfare are not carnal but mighty in God for pulling down strongholds, casting down arguments and every high thing that exalts itself against the knowledge of God, bringing every thought into captivity to the obedience of Christ, and being ready to punish all disobedience when your obedience is fulfilled."
—2 Corinthians 10:4-6 NKJV

Nine

Scepter Of Righteousness

I confidently acknowledge that I am walking upon Promise Land soil! He has landed my feet upon the rock!

This past week and a half have been intense for me. His teachings are stronger than ever before. It is application time. I feel He is saying to me:

"Stephanie, trust Me with which all I have graced upon you. The battle is yours. You have already won."

I saw the "SCEPTER"

It was lifted high as it was raised in front of me at church service this morning!

I have been granted ... all authority!

The Still Small Voice

"Lord,

"How gracious You are that You have given me access into my Inheritance today. As we continue to walk together, light my path and bless my footsteps. Amen."

Meek beyond words,

Stephanie

Ten

Miracle Healing

"We found power as one. Knitted together, moving as one. We are an unbreakable cord that God has joined together—for His purpose and His glory."

I asked the Lord for "truth," especially over Patrice's life. On our way traveling to the Turnaround Conference, the Lord put on my heart this word: "Affirmation."

We would not break the three-stranded cord under any power other than Jesus'!

We would watch over His sheep diligently, until He arrived and gave her a miracle!

We did not know we were on an assignment from God! We were the ones chosen by Him. He was the one who orchestrated this appointment and assigned us to carry it through, because we were willing participants, obedient in the Lord, and just in love with His daughter.

"Lord, thank you for graciously allowing us to stand in love with Patrice, and before You."

This is what the Father can accomplish with love and the willingness of hearts, by faith! I have learned that when love pours out, there is incredible strength in it.

I kissed God while standing in worship. I also saw a trumpet and opened my mouth and warm honey poured in. It went all the way to my tummy! It was very warm. I could actually feel it run down into my body. This was a first! I got drunk again ... in the spirit!

This was the Feast of Tabernacles!

Our faith has action. A fresh infusion of faith is what we are getting this weekend, here at Chavda Ministries!

They talked about the Overcomer Spirit. Colossians 3:1 says, "If then you were raised with Christ, seek those things which are above, where Christ is, sitting at the right hand of God." We have been raised with Christ. It is idolatry if you choose church culture over Bible scripture. Shout a joyful noise to the Lord!

We worshiped so much that we all got knocked into drunkenness the very first night! I had gotten a sore throat overnight and had been taking many throat lozenges. So, after the morning session on Friday, I exited the row and pointed to my throat and gestured for someone to pray for me. An usher did and just touched me ever so slightly with one finger ... and down I went! I could not hold it. I began to laugh because I still had a Hall's cough drop in my mouth! I got up and said, "Why I am having this?" and threw away the lozenge! I had absolutely no pain. I was healed!

The Still Small Voice

It's the desperate who will see the turnaround!
-Robert Stearns

But the most amazing healing I ever witnessed happened to Patrice! I knew her left hip was hurting her. Gently, I put my hands on her and prayed. On Thursday's arrival, they gave us a room at the far end of the hotel. We knew she was having a horrendous time trying just to walk upright. So, I requested a change in the location of our room to make it a bit easier for her. While a new room was being prepared, we all went to Wal-Mart. It was a Super Center, so I suggested to Patrice that she use the electric chair since she was in so much pain. We took pictures and had lots of giggles together. (Something prompted me to take the pictures). Later, it would be used by God! I didn't want to humiliate her by offering the photos, but God had a plan that was later to unfold for us— something tangible for us to testify with! Unknown to us, He would use us as a vessel to heal someone!

On Saturday night while in church, they called for healing for people with one leg shorter than the other. I did not hear them calling for this, but I knew Pat stood up. I thought it was for just leg problems. So, she went up and got slain in the spirit and landed on the floor after they prayed for her in the front line. She came back to our row afterwards, and the lady sitting in front of me tilted her head back to me and whispered out of the side of her mouth to me. She suggested she should sit with her leg up.

I questioned, "Now?"

The Still Small Voice

I said, "Maybe later."

Unannounced to me, I had no clue of what was happening or about to manifest, I was put on automatic pilot of obedience! I told Pat to sit with her leg up. But she automatically sat and stretched out her legs. The lady in front told me to tell her to put both legs up. I whispered out of the side of my mouth and asked, "Now what?"

I looked back at her in a "secrecy anointing" of instruction! She told me to hold both ankles and pray over them. She said, she couldn't do it because of respect for church policy there. So, my husband was standing behind me, and I motioned for him to lay hands on Patrice's ankles and help me pray. Our friend was standing behind Patrice, supporting her back. It was like she was in labor! I pulled on the right leg and prayed. ... Hum, hum, hum-dala ... nothing happened.

So I tried again ... praying ...hmmmmmm ... grow! Comical did you say? Yes, and then some! I know I can't heal anyone!

Then I just gave up and gave it to the Lord. I surrendered in self-weakness, "Lord, I don't know what to pray for or even what to do, but You do. So I am asking You to do what needs to be done here and heal her."

He had me open my eyes and I saw the left leg grow out about two inches, then the right leg moved out, then the left got jealous and moved out again at least two more inches! My husband jumped back and yelled, "WHOA!" In shock, he landed in the next row of seats!

The Still Small Voice

I began to cry and said to my husband, "Oh my God, did you see that?" We were all in shock! All around us, people were watching! We had made a scene when we jumped back in fright and amazement as we saw her leg actually grow out instantly in front of our eyes!

She wanted to write on a comment card what happened, but my spirit was so excited about this, I knew we had to share what just happened! I kept raising my hand half way up, in shyness, and distracting the pastor. He finally acknowledged me, "Do you have something to say?" he asked.

I cupped my hands and exclaimed in joy, "Her leg just grew out!"

He said to someone closer to him, "What did she say?"

The whole section in front of us said to him in unity, "Her leg grew out!"

He quickly jumped back to us and said, "Come up here!" Patrice walked up and gave her testimony in front of everyone! We rejoiced so loudly and gave all glory to God!

Absolutely amazing is the only way I can describe what had happened. After witnessing this, I would not be surprised to see a person come back to life after dying! I know what God can and will do.

Patrice then ran back and forth through the sanctuary on her perfect legs! Her whole body was working in total unity! I took videos of her and shared this with friends!

God gave us a before and after picture of His healing. Now the sequences came together and all the "whys" made sense! He brought the four of us here, He arranged the hotel, the shofar, had Patrice sit in the wheelchair, gave us special seating, and prompted us to be called out for healing by the pastor! Wow!

Now we know why God sent His chosen ones here and why we were joined together. It was all for our loving friend, Patrice! God protected her with a loving family, who wanted only to love and honor her, and see her healthy. He certainly delivered!

"A mustard seed of faith … moved Him"

What an incredible experience we had this weekend. God moved in all of us in amazing ways!

A three-stranded cord never fails, and it uplifted a sister to heights of honor that overjoyed Jesus. We are personally grateful to Christ and boast of His glory weekend here!

"My God Heals"

"Lord,

"You are spectacular!"

Amazed,

Stephanie

Eleven

No Longer Lukewarm

On our travel along the marshland, my husband and I talked about how we took notice of other church members who were living in their assignment, and totally with the Lord. We love seeing people living it out—His living words in completeness—not limited by anything of this world.

Our conversation continued and my husband went on to say, "Your writing time about God has taken a large consumption of your time, but we still need to be aware and not let go of and dismiss everyday life obligations."

We kind of let go lately. Whoa! "Thank you Lord, our focus is on You!" There is nothing I can do in the flesh or apart from Him anyway. So, He is in control right now, not me or us. He is providing for us in all the earthly ways.

We choose to know who He is and along this beautiful journey uncovering depths of Him, He is taking care and

taking over all of our cares and needs! He truly is ... as we turn our hearts toward Him!

It was 9:45 a.m. As we reached the bottom of the bridge over the intercoastal waterway, the Lord then placed this vision upon me:

I saw myself with my arms outstretched. Right above the world where I ascended, I could see I was in a white gown and my feet were hanging with my toes pointed downward. And I lifted off, like a soft air balloon that gently glides through the atmosphere. It appeared, as if showing me one foot in the spiritual realm, and the other leaving the earth. But my feet never even scraped or dragged on the surface of the world. I looked down to my right, and then left side. I saw how much I had ascended above and viewed the world below for what is. Full of sin. "I hate the world and everything in it," I kept repeating. Sin was all I could see and He raised me out of this. I said, "Wow, look where I am at! How high, ... and wow ... how did I get here?"

The Lord had made me whole, coming into alignment with Him!

No longer would I be of the world.

Psalm 97:10 NIV says, "Let those who love the Lord hate evil, for He guards the lives of His faithful ones and delivers them from the hand of the wicked."

Coming back home, we stopped in the grocery store. We were at such peace and total tranquility—just gleaming with

The Still Small Voice

love. As we checked out at the register, my husband saw it was drizzling lightly with rain. It was a very soft, gentle mist. He told me, "Wait here with the cart and I will get the car to pick you up."

I responded, "Yes sir," affectionately.

An older man saw this as he approached to enter the store, and said with a smile, "That sounds like a pretty good deal." I agreed as I found the delight in my heart. Perhaps a lost manner in today's society, but with hopes of a great comeback ... including opening doors for the ladies! Throughout the day, people gave us favor, stared at us with curiosity in their faces, delight in observing us, etc. I asked the Lord what was going on? He then showed me Himself and His arms extended and moving outwardly and He said, "Contagious."

This man saw my husband and I honor one another, and Jesus flowed onto others through us. I shared this with my husband as we drove away. My husband gleamed with joy and peace swarmed His heart!

All I know is this: "When you stand in the righteousness of God, there is strength and power." (I heard this in my spirit.)

What a day in Him this has been! I am on such a glorious high. I believe the prophecy I received in the July conference (pour out your spirit) has come to fruition. It never appears as you expect ... it's even better! This is such a monumental day!

The Still Small Voice

On our way home, after our Wednesday night worship and Bible study, I knew we had the anointing of the Holy Spirit covering us. I had been led to take authority over generational curses. Taking down strongholds and receiving freedom cleared a way for His identity to take residence in me!

When I had asked the Holy Spirit for His words of truth over this situation, I heard this:

> *"The riches are for you. I will drop them on you abundantly."*

"I thank You, Lord, for the works You have done in me. I am so humbled and grateful for the seal You have place upon me. Amen."

In a twinkling of an eye,

Stephanie

Twelve

Rose Of Sharon

I awoke today with a feeling of gladness and joy. I don't know if I was awake, sleeping, dreaming, or had a vision! I don't know, but it was lovely.

I became the form of my painting, I was the rose. I had not yet begun to apply the paint for my new painting, but I remember thinking about the picture as I drifted off to sleep. I couldn't get it off of my mind.

I remember saying to my husband (who was sound asleep), "Ah, this is so beautiful. Can't you feel it?" I was lying in an "S" shape on my side. I felt so warm and flowing, as if I was liquid, moving in a directional flow. But this was something I had never experienced before. It was as if my body was the top edge of the rose petal—and I saw it! My body was the curves of the petals, from head to toe. I curled and moved like the shape of the petals! It was an unusual feeling and "liquidy"! It was so beautiful! Then I received words of knowledge: "Like living water," and I saw a river with clear, refreshing water flowing!

I asked, "Lord, what is this?"

The Still Small Voice

He said, "Rose of Sharon."

My heart was filled with an overwhelming peace.

I shared this unique experience with my sister-in-law, who is a newly-born again Christian of just four months. She hesitated on the other end of the phone, saying "Steph, wait a minute, I think I know what this is ... you are the paint, and God is the painter."

God gave her the understanding! I was the liquid paint and He was using my body. I moved like fluid paint, just soothing and flowing along, as if in the river!

Just then I was given a download and I saw a large wooden paint brush handle. As my eyes moved down, I saw a round brush with a large amount of liquid paint dripping from it. It was a bright red color. Is this His blood that cleansed my soul?

I have enjoyed this pleasant experience with God. It has shown me how fun God is, and how He could use His imagination! Cool Beans! I have since then finished my watercolor ... He even gave me the scripture, Matthew 6:22:

> *"The eye is the lamp of the body, if your eyes are good, your whole body will be full of light."*

"Lord, You are *sooooo* much fun!"

Stephanie

Thirteen

When Something Ends ...

When something ends, it creates space for something new!

Tonight was our last night of Scroll Scribes Book Club. I will surely miss it. We were asked how the club affected each of us, and I felt such gratitude towards Anne, for listening to God to start this club and make it available. She invested a lot of personal effort, generated much excitement, and organized many guest speakers to enrich the experience. But even more, I am so grateful that joining this club gave me the motivation to write my first story. I was given a message that ***I would write a book*** about two years after I got saved. I have had questions many times over the years concerning what would I write about? I didn't believe I had "writing skills" or a burning desire in this area.

So, participation in the Book Club encouraged me to move forward to write the magnificent story about my

mother's gift to me! We were given an assignment to write a short story in one of our meetings. After five years of procrastination, I have finally committed it to paper! I shared this precious story with our group, and hopefully it will be published for the general public. The title is, *"When Heaven Meets the Mail."* It is dedicated to Stella McDonnell. (I love you, Mom.)

I also know now, that my journal will be my book that was to become a best-seller (...kidding around)! But, I kept getting titles for books throughout the year. I finally realized this past month that the journal I have been writing for two and a half years, is "The Book." Without conscious awareness, my journal that I have been writing with the living God would become my first book that was to be shared with many others.

I pray that God covers me with grace over what I have written and may this journey continue on to another book. May all who read it, delight in it, come to know God, and be transformed themselves into His image, through their own relationship with God. I will publish it next year and have it distributed around the world! This is a personal journey toward knowing God intimately and sharing my transformation, one day at a time, to be cleaned up and ready to fulfill my assignment! I know He is interested in each one of us and wants a deeper relationship with all of us.

So, now that I have committed that, He has put a burning desire in me to paint. I brought in three paintings. I realize that through this experience this past year, I have obeyed

The Still Small Voice

and He is ready to take me to the next thing. Revelation Painting!

I will dearly miss our group. We have shared so much of what God has been doing in our lives in this area. I found it very interesting that God had a unique assignment for each one, no two alike! It was many different projects, but one commonality. All for the body of Christ. Amen.

Bittersweet ending that opens to a fresh new chapter,

Stephanie

The Still Small Voice

"There is a time for everything, and a season for every activity under the heavens."

—Ecclesiastes 3:1 NIV

Fourteen

Crown Upon My Head

An unexpected graduation day has arrived for me today ... I found freedom!

I was on my treadmill in the early afternoon and I closed my eyes and began speaking in tongues. Next, I saw myself in front of our congregation, speaking in my prayer language. I had my eyes closed and I took the people on a journey into His heavenly realm.

I saw a new day of light. It was a beautiful orange sun. It was turning into yellow as it burst open and engulfed all the territory. It was warm and inviting. It then slowly became whiter and whiter, until His face appeared. Oh, Lord! Being in His presence is like no other place I have ever been in my mind or compares to any physical place you have ever experienced. Just close your eyes and seek Him. He will take you on a journey. He delights in you so much!

He led me into the throne room and I became child-like. As I played around His "Enormous Royal Chair," I peeked up from around the side with innocence and curiosity.

I saw His crown!

It is stunning! Well-crafted, brilliant gold, and filled with magnificent, enormous gems. God gave me a glance at one of the stunning stones up close, as it magically came out of its setting and presented itself in front of me. It was a marvelous pink and had incredible facets which revealed the beauty and brilliance. Its intricate beauty was inexpressible! I have never seen this color or this stone anywhere here on earth!

Next I was sitting on His lap and looking up at Him. I asked if I could try it on! I saw Him smile gently. He took the crown off and placed it above my head. I reached up for it with my small hands, while sitting on His lap. As I began to place it on my head, it went completely over my head, too large. He giggled. It then passed over my whole body. While I tried to hold the base of it, I realized just how enormous it was. I suggested He put it back where it belongs!

I took notice of how the Most High of authority saw this as a delight, and how He sits on His throne as a picture of love. His loving presence was enjoying His creation ... me! I then appeared as a tiny figure on His lap and was crying out:

"I love You! I love You, and I want to go everywhere You go. I could just hide between the folds of Your robe and no

The Still Small Voice

one would ever know I was there or even see me. I don't want to leave You. I want to be with You."

Then I spoke and sang in my spiritual language. Incredibly, I heard the whole place (heavenly realm) rise up with singing, in a diversity of exquisite languages. What beauty there was in listening to the sounds which honored Him, and exalted Him with love and majesty! It made me weep. My joy was filled with such an inner velocity that it projected through as a genuine fragrance of sweet oil.

"Oh Lord,

"Such beauty I have beheld. I love You! I love you ... and ... I just love You!"

Thank You, Lord for loving me,

Stephanie

The Still Small Voice

*"From Zion,
perfect in beauty,
God shines forth."*

—*Psalms* 50:2 NIV

Fifteen

Dying Of Self

I realized that I was slain in the Spirit last night! I have been under His presence since Sunday night in order to experience many lessons. This has given me great humility. I couldn't move last night, and I was in a special place with Him for three days!

It began last Sunday. I felt I didn't handle a situation as I should have. I know there was a better way, but what was it? I know I spoke right, but my heart wasn't right. I struggled with this for some time with anger, confusion, fear, jealousy, etc. I struggled until the Lord delivered me from it and spoke:

"I have positioned you next to your husband."

Though I am in the correct place (even while someone was so jealous and fearful that they didn't want me in the picture), I knew what was happening. I knew the sin and whys, but the Lord was having me soak in this, until I changed.

The outcome was to love on him (the jealous person) anyway.

"It's my way," the Lord said to me.

I am not to teach, correct, or do anything else the Lord hasn't told me to do. He will convict that person, not me. I am to stay in peace, because He is in control. Whoa! Huge lesson. The truth replaced the lie that wanted to separate us and cause strife. He kept me in His loving presence until I came to my right mind. It wasn't about the other person changing. God was after my heart.

I was in this present state for all of Monday, all the way up until I went to school that night. During worship, I began to cry with the burden, feeling the helplessness of the unsaved and sinners. I had not understood that I was experiencing intercession ... for the first time!

I saw a cute, red bird house with a bird flying toward it on the left. God took me back to the birdhouse and made visible to me the seed inside of it. As I peered through the opening, it was the food of life!

I pleaded with the Lord with heartfelt sorrow, "I will stand in for them, the lost. No, don't let them perish, they are Your creation."

This was the first time I felt like this. The presence of God and the pain just tore me apart, like the feeling of contractions. I wanted to leave the room and go downstairs in private where I could let go and cry my heart out in pleading, it hurt so deeply. Holding in the reality of what others may think of me if I let it go, a deep wailing of grief welled up within me. Tears rolled down my face with anguish.

I shared this with a prayer group at the end of class. I first asked the Lord if I should share. All three people had a word for me. One told me that last year I was on the milk, now I am getting the meat. Another said that the Lord's hand was heavy on those who carry the burden. We are to take them to the cross. With this I understood what the heaviness upon my head was during the last two days. I thought it might be the evil one and heard it was God teaching me something so valuable. Then the last person said, "You will know when to say something and He will instruct you. Listen."

The Lord instructed me to walk over to one member, because she had something more for me. And she did! It was huge! She said, "I did the same thing all day on Christmas Eve, I cried all day for the same reason. I was grieving for them too."

Whoa! That's when I realized what I was feeling ...

I was grieving!

I was grieving for the lost, the sinner, and the unsaved. I could only put my head low and stand in meekness, as I still am, of the awesome revelation teaching the Lord did. He wanted me to experience this, to know it. Not by mere words, but true divine conviction of the heart. I was feeling what Jesus was feeling.

Tuesday, while still in the spirit, I took a shower. I was praying and His presence engulfed me there, my secret place! I spent time with Him to receive all He was teaching me. With a passionate heart, I continued and asked for Him to search me for any defilement present in me. I told Him, "I will deal with it if you reveal it to me. I can't see what You can. I want to be clean." I crave Him. I don't care about the world and want to serve Him for the rest of my life. I give all, for the fullness of His purpose and destiny for me while on this earth. I don't want to wait any longer. I want to live for His intent.

I heard these words: "Pride, arrogance, self-seeking." This brought me to my knees in the shower. It hurt so much. I felt embarrassed and mortified. I sank to the drain. I repented, and asked forgiveness, took authority and disposed of it. Then the filling came. How sweet! For the rest of the night I could hardly move. It took me until today to come out of it. I was slain in the spirit for the entire night. But the meekness and pure humility swelled inside of me to encompass every pore. The quietness and stillness brought me into humbleness beyond comparison. The vastness of His being overcame and took territory in me.

The Lord showed me that He even loved the sinners, and so would I! I am turned inside out by the exposure and have been chosen to love the unlovely. Now I have am cleansed by His blood and forever more like Him. I know I'll never be the same, but better.

Your Empowered One,

Stephanie

Sixteen

The Lord Is On My Treadmill

I decided to have a very frank, honest conversation with the Lord this morning while walking on my treadmill.

Twelve years ago, when I moved here, it was given to me in my spirit that I would write a book. I always wondered why I had this inclination, and I would often ask myself, "Write a book about what?" I had a lot of ideas, but nothing obvious stared me in the face, or stirred in me a burning desire. I often pondered what He meant by this assignment, especially since the inclination never surfaced before (although I had always loved English in school).

Prompted by the Holy Spirit while walking, I asked:

"Please Lord, I need to know from You. Is the journal I am writing going to be, "The Book"?

I saw Him take my arms, wrap them around what appeared to be a journal and place it over my heart! Then as if I stepped away and looked at myself inside this picture, the journal appeared as a tablet with a spiral clip across the top, still wrapped in my arms, across my heart. Then I heard His gentle voice say:

"I have written these words on your heart."

My heart is overcome with love, and I gasp at this revelation, deeply touched by this moment with the Lord. Tears flood down my face as He finds a home in my heart. It reminds me of Moses and the tablet—God established His words in my heart. What can I say to these things? I am overwhelmed, I'm submerged in this present moment that He shares with me.

"Oh dear Lord,

"You are so good. Right now, there aren't any words that can describe what I am feeling at this moment ... no words."

I am blown away that the Lord took all this time for me to know Him intimately, and I didn't even know He was writing on my tablet—not a tablet of stone—but on my heart. I know there is scripture for this. It is familiar to me and warmly received. My Lord is above everything of this world. He is loving, patient, kind, good, gentle, caring, and a rewarder of those who diligently seek Him. He showed me today where He has placed Himself in me. I am grateful.

Always there, always cherished,

Stephanie

"Living Water"

Seventeen

I Need You

We had been preoccupied with selling our business and beginning another. As I stood motionless, I was struck by how much I missed spending time with the Lord. I longed for His clear presence and I missed the intimacy—even when I was without Him for only a day. I wanted Him to abide in me every moment. In order for me to function, my foundational operation was: **No division or separation from my Father, no matter what.**

So, feeling the distance that resulted from being overly busy, I told Him that I missed Him. I paused to listen and He was too quiet. "Lord? What is going on?" I asked.

Ever so gently He whispered, "Remember me?"

I sighed, but not in mourning or guilt. It was not sadness provoked by His question, but with gratitude. When I call upon Him, He is always there. I stood there, soaking in His presence. I breathed in deeply and slowly, listening for His voice.

The Still Small Voice

"You are in me," He said.

I noted He did not say, "He is in me," but instead, "I am in Him." I saw the huge covering of the Holy Spirit and little tiny me inside Him. I know in this moment that I am precious cargo! He made my soul aware of Who is operating in me and through me. He is magnified in size and power. I am one with Him and He is Deity.

Lifted up by this knowledge, my mind began to work independently for solutions without Him, and worry began to creep in. He corrected me quickly and I know I will bring all things to Him and not try to operate in my own strength. I clearly see that He wants to steer me. I grow increasingly aware of His great intentions and plans for me. I am secure knowing that He has already mapped out everything. I don't need to worry. Worry wastes my energy and steals my focus. I will rest in Him and walk in obedience and grace. I need to live beneath His wings. If I will stay within, I will never have to do without!

As I get dressed and prepare for the day, I reached for my cell phone to open the Bible app. I search for a specific Scripture, the one from the Amplified Bible about the One who lives in me being greater than the one who is in the world. I look and look, but cannot seem to find it. "Oh well," I sigh and looked at the time. I need to finish up and head to work.

I proceed to close the app on my phone and the sought after Scripture pops up all by itself! I know this is

confirmation from God. He provided the correct scripture and made me victorious before I left for the day! I am determined to walk in His victory. The awakening of truth today has clicked within me and transcended everything that I believed before. I have been truly moved into a new foundation that has bound me to Christ's blood within my heart and mind.

Little children (you belong to Him) and have (already) defeated and overcome them (the agents of the antichrist), because He who lives in you is greater (mightier) than he who is in the world.

—1 John 4:4 AMP

Totally belonging to You,

Stephanie

"For I am convinced that neither death nor life ... neither height nor depth ... will be able to separate us from the love of God that is in Christ Jesus our Lord."

—Romans 8:38-39 NIV

Eighteen

Clear Access

I am not alone following God's voice! Amen again and again. "Lord, I stand and rejoice in my husband having clear discernment of You, as You whisper into his ear!"

My husband is now telling me what God is saying to him during the day! It is happening more often than not! For the past several months, I have seen the gradual steps become a clear direction. I am so excited for him. I can see the joy upon his face! He is totally tuned in—listening and seeking the Lord. It's fabulous! As his wife, I stepped out of the way. Instead of trying to find the correct answer or feeling responsible for the decisions, I directed him to pray and seek the Lord for answers. This was difficult, but I heard in my spirit that I had to be in submission to the Lord in order for my husband to have **clear access** to Him!

Now, I am neither the idol nor the teacher. He seeks the Lord with vigor and passion that will transform him into the marvelous creature of God's intention. I am overjoyed for him!

Being shifted into correct alignment with my husband positioned as the head, and knowing that he is functioning as the head—that he is walking in obedience and daily seeking the Lord for our household—is more precious than gold!

For him, the growth has been incredible as he takes one step at a time, having a sure footing on a solid foundation in the principles of God's kingdom. Where he once sought answers on his own, he now says that nothing can tear him away from the Lord. He is determined to seek and be with the Lord the rest of his days. The Lord has honored our obedience to diligently seek Him in all things, as He gave me the desire of my heart.

I finally have what God originally planned for me. I am humbled; in tears as I recognize the Lord's love and intention with the gift of my husband. To be joined by heaven and live on earth together as one in Christ is beginning to emerge with full impact. I solemnly swear that I will love my husband and honor him as God would have me do.

"Thank you, Lord, for convicting me to move aside so you could bless me with such an incredible Godly love from my husband. I ask that you tenderly watch over us, and bestow great favor and magnified love in your precious son, Leonardo."

Thank you Gracious Lord,

Stephanie

Nineteen

No Distractions

I recently e-mailed a close friend to pray for us, that we will not get distracted with the new business or that the business pulls us away from the Lord. I desire that we may always exalt Him in all things ... always! I want to depend on Him for even the small details, to be in His midst always. I want to have His peace, joy, and humbleness. May we glorify Him and be in His will always and forever. May we share His presence and His word with everyone we meet. May God bless this new business adventure and use as He wills. May we always stay as humble servants and be blessed immeasurably.

"Thank You, Lord, for this new path. We willfully commit to steadfast measure as we abide in You. Cover us in Your grace. Amen."

God's words are always uplifting!

I just completed reading Romans 5-7. Incredible! I understand things differently now, and I am a fine creature

... wow! Sin was put to death. Period. End of story. That sinful person is not who I am. I will turn to the Spirit within me and stay there. I can now recognize when I am away from that position. I know when the flesh has taken over, and it is not a pleasant aroma! I know He will do more in me and I am intently listening.

"Lord, we honor You. We thank You for this new season. We earnestly don't want to do just business—especially not the old way. You have put us in this mountain again: for the second time. We have stayed with You in prayer for the outcome and patiently waited for Your timing. We trust we will not have our way, but have a new, fresh, Godly kingdom way in all our deeds. We will not trust in ourselves, but be guided into all truth for this upcoming venture. May it be nothing like our first experience. *(We had asked God to take away our thriving business three years ago because of the unfulfillment we both acknowledged. We wanted more in life and we were willing to sacrifice it all for what He had for us.)*

"Lord, please show us how to own and manage a sanctified business. May we encounter many new ways, as You direct our steps. We are concerned that we may fall into some old traps set up against us, and we refuse to do the old thing. Make it afresh, Lord. Teach us what You wanted us to know the first time. We repent and put away our old hats, and put on the new You! Teach us, Father. We will be like little children, hungry to be fed by our Father, asking and listening for divine ways.

The Still Small Voice

"**My old flesh will not reign. Cut it away so all that remains, is You.**

"This is going to be very interesting, Lord. We both love You so much. We confidently apprehend all that awaits us. We boldly step into what lies ahead as we place our complete trust in You. Amen."

Lovingly,

Stephanie

The Still Small Voice

"For sin shall no longer be your master, because you are not under law, but under grace.

—Romans 6:14 NIV

Twenty

Strawberry Fields

Who would have thought God would use a Strawberry farm to teach a lesson?

I jumped at the idea of picking strawberries when a friend announced on Facebook that she was going. She invited friends to pick the fields with her on opening day of the season.

It seemed early to me for strawberries to be ready to pick, and I thought maybe they were in a hot house. So off we went on our adventure to the farm!

We arrived just as our friends were leaving, her two beautiful, energetic young children in tow. How comical it was to observe their freedom to be children. Love and joy saturated the van with whimsical laughter. No, not theirs … ours!

We spent a few minutes and became acquainted with the owners before setting off with a smile and our buckets. As

we began our trek, we had a game plan. We set a pattern to cover the large field. Within about fifteen minutes we noticed most of the strawberries were scarce and not quite ripe. But we pursued each row on a mission. We were like two little children on a quest to find the hidden ruby red berries. We stopped for a moment to see a nearby donkey and some sort of "steer-like" animal. Believe me, although I enjoy this, I am not a farm hand and would fail a test on farm animal distinctions!

I remember breathing in deep and feeling the freedom and joy of just being in the outdoors. There was a slight breeze and it was a comfortable, sunshiny day. As we made our way through the rows, finding few berries, I exclaimed, "Okay, let's go!" I was done. Something came over me and I acknowledged we were not to pick just for the sake of picking. They weren't ripe enough yet. It was okay to stop and wait. I had this overwhelming thought that I wanted to honor their farm. I wanted to allow the berries to ripen so everyone could enjoy them. Though I was enjoying the lovely day, I did not want to pick the berries prematurely.

I decided to go find a bench (or preferably a rocking chair) and just drink in all the farm had to offer. There was such an atmosphere of peace and relaxation. I wasn't ready to leave. Something inside of me let me know to stay a while longer in this beautiful place with my husband. We joked about the quantity of picking vs. quality! He won the prize for the most berries picked. I humbly pointed out that they were

supposed to be red, not green in color! No competition, but fun observation. It was a kind way of saying ... "Time to go!"

We were having a nice, comfortable conversation with the owners as they shared their future ideas of expansion with tourism. A lady came into the quaint, log store and said, "They are not ready to pick yet. I sure hope they are ready next week for the strawberry festival." So, I had the opportunity to pray out loud and declare rain and sunshine for the fields with God's blessing. How awesome to be able to bless a farm! It was the first time for me. I spoke prosperity over the strawberries and a pronounced a great festival for the next week. "Gee," I thought to myself, "I'm becoming bold!"

We left and meandered down a dirt road that weaved through the farm. There alongside of us we witnessed what I call, "The dance of the bulls!" One was calling to the other ... way over yonder in the next fenced area. As the bulls sounded off and pawed the grass with their hooves, all the other cows totally ignored what I found intriguing.

The field was filled with cows eating grass. They looked just like the cows my mother and father use to point out to me as we traveled the roads of America! "Look Stephanie, moo cows," she used to say with an enthusiastic voice. Just watching them stirs pleasant childhood memories of my family for me. My memory of going to a farm and buying fresh milk was a weekly ride with my sisters and brothers. I cherished those wonderful days with my parents and

carried on this tradition with my own daughter! Reflecting on this and being able to share the wonderful stories brings great joy to my heart.

As we were leaving, my husband observed the tranquility he felt today. It was a fresh breath of air—a moment of total relaxation, free from the burdens of the world. I instantly realized the plan God had for us today.

It's in the hidden things. God told me that the fields were not ripe yet. He spoke to me that the harvest was not yet ready for picking. The berries needed time to mature. He told me to wait for the right timing. To be patient. They will be there. I needed to rest in Him.

"Oh Lord, I guess if you can if you can speak through a donkey, you certainly can speak through a strawberry field! Oh, how You love me! Thank You for the lesson today. I will wait. It's not time yet. I need the maturing and lessons. How grateful I am that You would take the time to show me this in such a lovely way. Lord, whatever it takes, I am willing to go through it. No matter how hard it seems, I know that it is You who is training me for reigning. I don't want to go ahead of the harvest of souls, as You ripen me! Help me, oh Lord, to be patient and wait for the full ripening."

With enduring rich love,

Stephanie

Twenty-One

Come Walk with Me

Once again I find myself feeling frustrated. We are trying to run this company, but I feel at odds again! I wanted to orchestrate the plan, but it was turned around and now the plan is how someone else has chosen to see it. I thought my way was great and worked well. "How could he do this to me?" I thought. The system was working just fine before he decided to do it his way. We are in a complete difference of opinion about this. So, I decided to pull back and sit in the parking lot of these villas and just steam! Okay, that wasn't going to help anything or anybody. In fact, it would not solve my dilemma, it would only make things worse. "I know what I'll do," I said, "I will talk to God about it." And so, I did …

"Lord, I am so angry. I am frustrated about all of this," I began.

Before I could say anything more, He spoke to me gently and said, "Come, walk with me."

He took me to the beach, and I was watching as the vision unfolded. He was in a white gown and I stood next to Him. I was just 25 inches tall! You see, I was a child! He took my left hand and we walked together quietly along the ocean. I didn't hear Him say anything, but I know He talked with me. The place turned into what looked like a sand desert. It was just Him and me.

How beautiful of my God! He removed all my anxieties and anger as He whispered, "Relinquish it."

I became so peaceful and content. It is amazing how in an instant, He changed me again. I felt such tranquility, such love.

"Lord, I am beyond words ... other than, I love You so and thank You for loving me so much. You are the answer. I love you with all of my heart, with all of my being. I am humbled, and will always remember this day. Amen."

Okay, I am ready to go back to work, but now it will be with Him. As I breathe Him in, I am relaxed and full.

Your child,

Stephanie

Twenty-Two

Wisdom in a Breakthrough

What a valuable lesson I learned today. I truly got a breakthrough! As I stammered with frustration and anger at my husband, I behaved like an ornery child wanting candy in the check out at the grocery store. All because I didn't get my way!

Sound familiar?

Yep, even though I am an adult, today I acted like an out-of-control, screaming, kicking, selfish child. I believed on all accounts ... I am right. I am righteous! How dare he (my husband) not see it my way? Why is he so stubborn? Why doesn't he change? He's not getting it! He's being mean to me! What's wrong with him? I'm right, doesn't he get it.

But even through all of this anger, I knew I needed help. I didn't want anyone to see me like this (like it wasn't obvious) I walked into my church with my plastic smile on. I walked in and around the corner, coming face to face with, yep, the pastor's wife! "How are you?" she asked with a genuine smile.

"Fine," I said. my face looking like a constipated dog's face!

Oh dear, I thought. My *long running perfect streak is over!* Miserably, I blurted out, "No, I'm actually not fine."

Politely, my pastor's wife asked what was wrong. I told her with as much restraint as I could manage, "I am so angry at my husband!"

Compassion spoke within her voice, "For what?" she asked.

At that moment I realized I didn't have a simple clear answer, so I dug deep. "Because he is not loving me the way he should be. I have peace and he doesn't!" Wow! It sure didn't appear that way by my actions!

It was time for the Holy Spirit to step in and for me to step out! In that moment I was convicted about letting go of my expectations and allow God to minister to my husband. I needed to stop being a teacher and release him (and myself) from me. The Lord wanted to teach my husband for Himself and I wasn't so comfortable with not standing in the doorway in this area. Although I had wanted my husband to be strong in the way of the Lord, the revelation had to come by the renewing and restoration that comes only by the Holy Spirit—not through another party's experience. For my husband to be guided into all truth, he needed intimate relationship with the Holy Spirit—without me to meddle.

I loosed my husband and he became bound to God. This was a beautiful moment, but a blind one for me to see until I set down my pride and the Lord set me up with a divine, unscheduled appointment!

I choose to honor my husband and respect him. I can turn my expectations over to God. For we are not to control one another or hold fault with our brothers and sisters in Christ. I am sure glad of the seven times seventy provision! Quickness in forgiveness lays the pathway to revitalization. It restores us on His pathway of redemption. Grasping how many times He has forgiven me, is an eye opener to humility.

Having a mature Christian speak into your life is a special blessing. This day I began a new chapter in my marriage—a righteous marriage lived out heaven's way. **What a glorious day it has been!**

"Lord, how humbled I am that You made this divine appointment for me today. This has set me free and our marriage has taken a positive turn to became a covenant marriage in respect of Godly principles. Pour out Your blessings upon us. Capture the very essence of Your sweet fragrance. Teach us to have the greatest marriage ever known. Amen."

Gratefully,

Stephanie

The Still Small Voice

"Mercy and lovingkindness and truth have met together; righteousness and peace have kissed each other."

—Psalm 85:10 AMP

Twenty-Three

Lack of Knowledge

"My people perish for lack of knowledge."

God is my constant source. He never runs out or runs dry! I can keep going to Him for **all** things. I am beginning to know what I have inherited from God. I am indebted to love!

The beauty inside of me is beginning to be revealed. I am learning that all He is … is truly in me. I am learning that neither Jesus nor His gifts are sitting in heaven, waiting for me to pick up later. It is hidden in me, available, and revealed to me as I inquire and seek the Holy Spirit to reveal Jesus to me. Through trials and tribulations I have come to see and know truth. These tests enlighten me and bring me to the heights of who He is—fullness and truth. Amen.

As I am convicted of this in my spirit, I treasure this newfound truth. For there is nothing lacking in me!

I went through several trials while guests were in town. As I struggled, I looked up into His face, with my hands folded and saw Jesus on the cross. I said with true humility, "Forgive them Father, for they know not what they do." I am being tormented by confusion and through all evildoers, who obey the dark one. This was revealed to me spiritually to awaken my hurting soul. No longer will I resent or be afflicted by this trickery. The evil one comes to kill, steal, and destroy.

I was being dishonest with myself. Throwing darts back was not lady-like! Retaliation is not the answer. What I truly wanted was for them to love me and spend time with me voluntarily. I decided that emotions were not going to dictate to me any longer. I had a true divine turnaround today! My bruised heart will not go ahead of me and have me say or feel things that may hurt others or myself. It is no longer a point of entry for the enemy to distract me. For my battle is not against flesh. I will no longer be moved by what I see.

I am not dependent upon anyone's turn-around or apology to me. I am going to submit to God. I will also forgive myself and come in right standing with God. I heard in my spirit that I am to lead by example, by the Holy Spirit. I will choose to pray for others and not be offended. I will not try to be the Holy Spirit for others. I

will forgive. Forgiveness does not excuse bad behavior or stamp approval on mine. But what it will do is this:

"The truth will set you free, for the truth is in the heart. It's where I dwelt in the Spirit. It's where My spirit is. It's my dwelling place" (I heard in my spirit).

"Lord, I am Increasingly grateful for the expansion of who I am in You and what is available to me through the cross and Your life in me. Lord, I will stay under your wings and be a blessing to others.

"For my battle is not against flesh and blood, but against principalities and dark spirits. I will choose to love those whom You first loved also. Regardless of my emotional state or preferences, I will not judge the wounded and have loving mercy as you have done for me. 'For we often gauge another person's life, based upon our own.' Retaliation is no longer on the docket ... love is."

Gratefully,

Stephanie

"His mercy and grace endures forever"

The Still Small Voice

"And you will know the truth, and the truth will make you free."

—John 8:32 NIV

Twenty-Four

My Father's Daughter

As we worshipped in church this morning, the Lord hovered over the congregation. The atmosphere was thick with His presence. He filled my soul with gladness and immersed me in His Spirit. Today I had the responsibility to greet, usher, and collect the tithe. What a spectacular position to serve and be able to bless others. There is such joy that comes with servanthood. I immersed myself in His love as I worshipped Him in praise with singing with my arms lifted high. I opened my mouth to speak the words, "I am," He finished my sentence with, **"...my Father's daughter."**

I gasped with this heart-shaking revelation and I could not hold back the tears. I had always believed this to be true, but today this became absolute for me. I felt undivided—two became one. I saw Him above me and a direct line, like a tunnel, that connected us together. This moment was like no other. I felt like I was adopted by Him and this was never to be cut or broken. It was sealed in my heart today. Although I was always His, today I know for sure—I am in

my Father. It's my inheritance and true identity—to whom I belong to. This was official!

I just heard Him say I to me, **"I am well pleased."** My heart is humbly filled with satisfaction and tenderness at knowing this. My spirit jumps and I leap toward the Father's embrace.

"Lord, I fall to the deepest measure of my heart. Not just in overwhelming happiness, but with total awareness of Your sovereignty. How can I express in words what I feel? There are no letters, words, or utterances that picture Your indescribable love for me. Today I have received undeniable confirmation, that I am yours. Tears stream uncontrollably upon receiving this precious gift of adoption. As this pierces my heart with gladness, I pray …

"Thank You for giving me the right today to be called, 'Child of God.' Now we're family, so … Mi Casa, Es Su Casa!"

Your grateful, loving, humbled daughter,

Stephanie

"I am my beloved's, and his desire is toward me."
—Song of Songs 7:10 NIV

Twenty-Five

Loving Patience

As He works on renewing my mind this year, He brings to my remembrance some things from December ... He certainly has had His hands full with this one!

I believe that through these conflicts, God is definitely training me to turn my thoughts to Him. Willing, but uncertain just how to complete this turnover, He prompted me to bear witness. I heard:

"Just hold on a little longer ..."

This was whispered in my spirit at the onset of a thought that stirred my emotions. So, instead of acting upon the thought, or allowing it to take a negative root, I listened as He whispered again gently to me, "Hold on."

This intentional hesitation allowed me to filter in new thoughts of creation that perpetuated His divine truth! As I am faithful to abide in Him patiently, He gives me a new thought that exiles the previous one, in an instant! A

clear exchange was evident. The "old skin" was removed by seeking, under covenant of truth, to discover something "new." This allows a permanent elevation of thought!

> *"Our thoughts are not His thoughts, until we succumb our own thinking to His."*

He is undoubtedly training me up and refining me into pure, spun gold! My time has changed and there are many more challenges to face. If I am not pressing into Jesus, I can be redirected where I definitely don't want to be, either by my soul or by something else seeking to distract me from His purpose. So, this discovery is good. All the answers are with Him. Nowhere else. So, I am being disciplined by my Father at age ___ (Nay ... we won't fill in that blank)!

Even though this is not the most comfortable place to be in, it is a majestic one. I get to be with the Father, and that makes it all worthwhile. Amen.

> *"But seek first His kingdom and His righteousness, and all these things will be given to you as well."*
> Matthew 6:33 NIV

"Lord,

"I know there is a lot You are stirring in me right now. It has forced me to turn my eyes and mind to You. My thoughts are Your thoughts to be! I am still in training! I

relinquish each day to you, as I choose to be in You. I do love You dearly. Thank You for being patient with me and tender and tolerant as I grow. I weep because I know, there is no one else like that.

"Thank you, Lord, for circumcising my traditions and learned behavior of thinking and implementing Your ways and will.

"You are so merciful and forgiving. You never bring up my iniquities and rub my nose in them, You only reveal to me who You are in me and who I am in You. I am humbled as I stand here in awe of Your love for me."

Thank you Lord,

Stephanie

> "I'm grateful when the heat is turned up ... for it is in the refining fire that I am transformed into fine spun gold."
>
> Stephanie M. Lumbia

The Still Small Voice

"*Look among the nations! Observe! Be astonished! Wonder! Because I am doing something in your days—You would not believe if you were told.*"

—*Habakkuk* 1:5 NASB

Twenty-Six

Fishes and Loaves

Today was interesting to say the least. I worked in our cleaning business today with my husband who was clearly at the helm of this operation. We plunged in with gusto, but we knew from the start that we didn't have enough material to supply all our needs today.

I declared, "We will have enough and the Lord will supply it." After all, it is His business and we are just the keepers—the stewards. I stood in complete consecrated faith, knowing that He would handle this situation. Unwavering faith that took hold of me, like never before.

It was physically obvious that we were grossly short, undeniably to anyone who had eyes to see. We sincerely knew we didn't have nearly enough linen or towels to accomplish all the cleaning jobs lined up today for our housekeeping business. I remained steadfast in faith and encouraged my husband that all would be well. **What happened next was miraculous … and it happened right in front of us!**

We finished packing all our linen/towel bags for the quantity needed for each villa in three hours. We set them aside, and breathed out a sigh. Unconcerned about the problem, we went about the task at hand, not fretting. We focused diligently on what needed to be done and not our lack. When we finished, I gasped! My husband turned to me in astonishment and asked. "What?"

"Look!" I said. "There are still linens and towels on the shelves!"

The whole crew knew we didn't have enough when we began. But when we finished, we not only had enough ... there were supplies left over! In amazement, we stood motionless at the stillness in the atmosphere. Bewildered by what just happened, we knew that only God could have done this, with us believing in His provision. It kind of reminded me of the two fishes and five loaves of bread Jesus blessed and used to feed over 5,000 people!

As I write this, I hear Him say that the multitudes He provided for were not just fed, they were "**WELL FED!**" Like the fish and bread, our stock multiplied when it was offered up to God and blessed! Jesus instructed the disciples to feed the people with their hands, and the goodness of God never ran dry. They were not just filled, but filled to abundance, overflowing, and running over.

We had more than enough. And as I turned each time to reach for a bundle of sheets, it was as if I was at a drive through window and someone was handing them to me. I would take one and another would appear!

The Still Small Voice

I know this sounds crazy, but it is the honest truth. My husband and I are so amazed at what only God could have done. We are astonished and elated at the same time! Our Father multiplied our linens and towels today. How amazing He is. In the midst of our need He was the ultimate source of supply!

"Lord, You have clearly shown me what You can do with little. You not only supplied us, but even gave us more than we asked for, with leftovers! How great You are. How our faith is growing. I can't wait to share this with everyone I meet! You are magnificent! Not because You filled the order, but because when standing in faith and uncompromising dependency upon You, You are truly with us. Your love shines on everything we put our hands to. How beautiful You are. Thank You for letting me see the works of my Father today. I will rejoice and shout it on the mountain top! Our God reigns! Amen,"

Amazed at Your Greatness,

Stephanie

"Then the LORD your God will prosper you abundantly in all the work of your hand, in the offspring of your body and in the offspring of your cattle and in the produce of your ground, for the LORD will again rejoice over you for good, just as He rejoiced over your fathers."

Deuteronomy 30:9 NASB

The Still Small Voice

> "And my God will meet all your needs according to His glorious riches in Christ Jesus."
>
> —Philippians 4:19 NIV

Twenty-Seven

When Did I Enlist?

I have desperately been trying to get to my computer to make new entries in my journal, but not had any spare time. So, I am sinking into one thing that is so important for me.

The season of "busy" is here. Yesterday, I believe, was a big breakthrough for my husband! The Lord revealed that we were running a race to the goal line (football field) back in March. Since then, we have both been hit with heavy duty battle. I have entered near the ten yard line and can now see the length of the field I just ran! The Lord told me:

"I am strengthening you for the battle, for war."

Yikes! I really wasn't planning on enlisting in a war to start with. It would seem I have been drafted anyway! He recalls my memory to when I saw Jesus on the front stage at church. He was so large that I could see only His face peering out to the congregation! As He looked to and fro, I asked Him with deep concern, "Lord, what are you looking for?"

He answered, "My chosen ones—the ones who truly love Me."

I began to jump up and down, waving my arms wildly, yelling desperately, "Here I am, Lord, here I am ... pick me ... I love you ... don't pass me by!"

He said, "I see you!" I smiled as He acknowledge me, knowing my heart was all for Him!

Now, my husband is diligently seeking God to understand what is going on for him. This current trial is meant for his good. I know now that my husband is sure this is God's hand upon his life and that will bring him peace. I have been praying to have our Lord give my husband insight and revelation as to what he is to learn from the refining fire. He so desires to do more for the kingdom, it's where his true treasure lies. His yearning is to grow and know the destiny God has for him.

Yet, he didn't see God was already using him!

He (like me) thought he needed a clear picture to identify what God's hand upon our life looked like. He wanted something sure, without a mistake, to know that we were doing God's work and carrying out His plan rather than having our selfish ways and wants.

We need God's will and desire, and nothing short of **His** agenda is implemented into *our* lives. Not trying to have Him fit into ours. This is our true desire So ... as we walk ... we will learn!

Help us, oh Lord,

Stephanie & Leonardo

Twenty-Eight

Lion's Den?

I just have to share this interesting story that happened to me yesterday. I am still dismayed. It bothered me.

I feel like there was something unfinished, but my God made it complete today.

I shared this with a friend and chuckled at her response. She said exactly what the Lord said she would! "Ask the Lord to reveal it to you!"

I still ponder if this is an assignment or if I should just flee. Is it meant for me to learn discernment through this, or (as I hope), to save the people from the awful wrath? I have never experienced such obvious evidence of evil witchcraft over a group of people or a place. I often get my revelations in pieces and increments (unlike my husband who knows the outcome before it happens). He can access the whole truth at once, and without fail! This is a special gift from the Spirit. So, knowing this, I no longer feel unsettled about this situation, because my Father has revealed His purpose for me to know. How beautiful is our Father. How He cares for me. He knows how to handle me well!

Yesterday started out incredibly, that is right up until ... I went to a nail salon. I was surrounded by wolves, but I held steadfast. Later I realized that earlier in the day, I had put notes in my computer from Joyce Meyers' message, *"Armed and Dangerous."* The subject was, "Authority is all mine." My authority has been given to me by the same authority that rose Jesus from the dead. This same power lives in me. The power of the Holy Spirit came upon me, and I walked in a different light.

This is truly an empowering thought.

Boy, did I walk into the pit! But I didn't get bitten even though I had no influence there, or have the ability to change the atmosphere, I could only stop and cease the arrows. As I gripped the arm chair handles, my fingers turned blue from holding on so tightly during my pedicure. Feeling helpless, I experienced fear, and without my husband's protection, I felt alone.

Now, I sure wish I could have handled it better. It was an awful place to be. I was led in, unprepared for what was to come. I was out of my cozy comfort level, but I don't think I was called to change people. I wish I had a louder voice and did not feel fear when I am in this kind of position. If I had spoken, perhaps it could have impacted some people into the correct kingdom. I won't go back there anymore, although

this is my second time at that salon. It would be foolish to return to (what I described to my husband as) a dark cave. I thought I could stay peaceful and meek and just get my nails and toes done. Wrong! I didn't hear from God (other than after leaving) that there was a haughty spirit there. I was insulted by a technician about my appearance, and there was an undertone of sexual content: word-twisting, lust, and jealousy. They fought amongst themselves, there was tension, competition, anger, and total un-professionalism sank this tank. And to make matters worse, the customers were okay with all this controversy and disrespect. They just went about their business! Could no one else see what underlayment this sat upon? Was I the only one?

I wrote to my friend to help with the "unsettledness" I still felt the following day. Just then, it hit me. Wow! I quickly wrote back to her the revelation that came without me noticing it when I was writing to her previously! It seems as though when I write or speak to someone, the Lord reveals His truth to me. I can't figure it out, so He shows me.

I knew entered into a cave-like place (the salon) but He called it a pit! I <u>did</u> have authority because I came out unscathed and unbitten! Whoa!

I am given all authority!

This is a profound new concept of truth that was given to me today! I was shown the spiritual warfare going on in that place! This is the first time I have ever experienced seeing in the spirit—actually seeing the works of darkness

manifested in the physical atmosphere. But no one was fighting the enemy, there was only complacency. Actually, I witnessed a lot of anger amongst themselves, ripping each other apart, like a gang of wolves. I thought I was being too polite and honoring the people. But the Lord revealed to me to honor myself and the people, but not the demons. (This was something very new for me to hear from the Lord.) I must have honor for myself and be careful who I give it away to (not to give it so quickly). For if I don't take the authority over the darkness, it will continue.

I must be submissive to Him (Jesus) only!

God immediately put to use this power, established and surfacing in me today! It was like, whoosh! I didn't know what hit me because it came at me so fast! Perhaps I ducked when I was meant to fight, perhaps I was to do just exactly what I did. I have the Lord, and I walked in as an authority because they did bow down and hushed. Nothing could touch me and or devour me. It was like watching a movie, sitting on my throne chair with a bubble surrounding me! His majestic power was there and I was in Him witnessing what He wanted to show me today. Though I did feel helpless in the moment, I now see that the presence of God was in the room—they either had to back down or flee. He was larger and the "critters" were set lower than me.

I was looking to flee and escape the situation, but instead, I really got the power, just like Daniel in the Lion's Den!

The Still Small Voice

"Okay, God, the more I keep writing, the more you reveal to me. I get it!"

This has been an uncomfortable teaching, but powerful! I am finding out, WHO is in me. He is so much greater than anything in the world.

"Lord,

"I am so grateful and know that I am powerful from within. I have the Lion and the Lamb!"

Learning Every Day,

Stephanie

The Still Small Voice

"Daniel answered, 'May the king live forever! My God sent His angel, and He shut the mouths of the lions. They have not hurt me, because I was found innocent in His sight. Nor have I ever done any wrong before you, Your Majesty.' The king was overjoyed and gave orders to lift Daniel out of the den. And when Daniel was lifted from the den, no wound was found on him, because he had trusted in his God."

—Daniel 6:21-23 NIV

Twenty-Nine

Believe

As I traveled in my car to meet my husband at a café for lunch, the Lord talked to me. He had me preaching that morning as I stood before the mirror of my bathroom. I thought about the scriptures and all of a sudden, it felt as though all of the scriptures were inserted into me. I felt it go to my stomach! I knew all the scriptures! I mean, I *know* that I don't actually know them all, but it was as if the things taught to me by the Holy Spirit all suddenly aligned with scripture. It felt as though they were deposited into me, in one big gulp.

So, I meditated on this for a moment and asked the Lord, "Will I need these for preaching in the days to come? Will I be speaking about them and need to know them? Is this why You did that? Did You do it because I didn't know them and would soon have to? Oh, Lord, what am I to do with this?"

"Wait a minute," I reasoned with the Lord, "Esther didn't preach."

Then He showed me how Esther was bathed in perfume and beauty. (As I identified with her in a given prophecy.) I said back to Him, "She didn't use scripture or preach. What was so special about her that I will use?"

He answered, "INFLUENCE ... SHE HAD INFLUENCE."

Wow! I am learning to ask, and He answers!

I prayed with reverence and determination, "Lord, I want to be in the supernatural with You. I want to see the supernatural happen all around me on a continuous basis. I want the world to witness You. I want to see more of You and Your miracles."

So, while I was taking in the sunshine under an umbrella, with my husband and a capuccino, I had a conversation with the Lord. I asked Him, "Tell me about your Son, Jesus." He showed me the supernatural; the things He did. I asked to see them and He showed me (in my spirit) back when He turned the pitchers of water into wine at the wedding. He seemed to chuckle a little and said, "They didn't believe Him." I was shocked and said, "Why not? I would have ... Lord, I want to see them," I pleaded. "Please show me. Please use me and let the world see You."

I became child-like in nature as my Father brought me to this point in time. Funny how He does that, and often while I'm in public!

I took another sip then asked Him, "You made us. Why are we in doubt?" *(Knowing very well why and what happened in history.)*

I heard Him say, "Believe."

My heart came into alignment with His command. I find the miracles Jesus did believable. I trust in Him and all He is. There is no reason for doubting on my behalf. Perhaps it is because I'm not wanting proof before I believe. **I just believe!**

Love You through Every Day Life,

Starest

My new given name!

The Still Small Voice

"Therefore, everyone who acknowledges Me before men and confesses Me (out of a state of oneness with Me), I will also acknowledge him before My Father Who is in heaven and confess (that I am abiding in) him."
—Matthew 10:32 AMP

Thirty

If God be for Us

After a trying weekend, we received a three day "OFF" pass and transferred the responsibility of work to our newly positioned manager! My husband truly deserved a rest from a weary summer schedule. He had earned it!

We were looking forward to the respite, but it turned out to be anything but peaceful and restful. My husband is an achiever, and ambition drives his nature as well as mine. By the third day I had conceded into the boxing match of confrontation, irritation, and turmoil. So, how did this happen to us? How did we get caught in the snarls? We didn't have this on our menu plan! We planned a peaceful Sabbath rest with the Lord.

Desperate, I sent out a signal to God, "S.O.S!"

There are the times when you know you are in too deep, you acknowledge it, and call out for deliverance! All pride falls to the wayside, humility kicks in, and intense seeking and hearing accelerates. Peace becomes your warfare, and all victory becomes yours!

> *"What then shall we say in response to these things? If God is for us, who can be against us?"*
>
> Romans 8:31 NIV

"For we are more than Conquerors!"

Thursday evening when my husband asked me to go on a bike ride. Grudgingly, I said okay! Thoughts of foolishness swam in my head at the notion of spending more time together on the war path! But, confrontation with the true enemy was about to emerge and be put to a screeching halt. Words to others, if in battle with one another, try a different scenery!

We know that it is in our biking we spend time with God and get free! So, while I peddled frantically ahead of him, I finally looked up (because I was tired of looking down!) and said, "Lord, what is going on? Please help us," I pleaded with mercy. "Show me the truth. I'm angry and drowning here." And He did.

> *So shall My word be that goes forth out of My mouth: it shall not return Me void (without producing and effect, useless), but it shall accomplish that which I please and purpose, and it shall prosper in the thing for which I sent it.*
>
> Isaiah 55:11 AMP

The Still Small Voice

While still pedaling vigorously, I submitted to His holiness and He rapidly responded! I saw a pit. It became engulfed with snakes. So I began rebuking it (the darkness) out loud with authority. I commanded that it get behind me ... now! (Forgetting for the moment, that my husband was biking behind me!) I quoted Psalm 91. No foe can touch me and my enemies must scatter!

My husband asked me who was I talking to, as he passed me along my left side! "Oh, just the enemy," I said emphatically, with relief in my voice and a smile on my cheeks! Then I was drawn into the vision again, and saw a snake pit and a tail popped into view. "Oh, it's a rattle," I said calmly. Then quickly my spirit informed me as I spoke with discernment and questioned with deep concern, "A rattle snake?"

Then I heard in my spirit, again, "rattle." "He is trying to rattle me!" I exclaimed in heightened awareness! I took this in for a moment.

"He is trying to rattle me"—and as I pondered that thought for a moment, it became clearer. I took this in for a moment. I knew what the enemy was trying to accomplish.

The Lord showed me what the enemy was trying to do. He's just trying to rattle me—that is what he's up to? I broke into a big smile and began to chuckle while riding my bicycle! I trampled on him so quick; with a jolly hearty laugh at spoiling his antics. "How foolish thy plot is," proceeded confidently out of my mouth! I said, "I shall devour you!" Immediately my husband and I were completely released.

The coil was gone as well as the head and tail! The obstacle was removed from our pathway to righteousness! We were brought back into the alignment of reconciliation with one another, instantly! What the enemy meant for harm, God used it for our good!

When my husband caught the fullness of it, his eyebrows raised and his eyes opened widely and he asked me to repeat what I had just said! He revealed that he had almost the same dream the other night! We are apparently a big threat to the enemy. We overcame the wiles of the devil together, in complete joint efforts! I think this was the first time we had the same vision ... and the timing was almost simultaneous.

I believe God revealed what the two of us can do together in the power of the Holy Spirit. In cooperation with total dependency on God, He will keep us safe from the enemy's traps. We know who the counterfeit is. We are so full of the power of the Holy Spirit that no foe can have us. All victory is ours! We are learning our lessons and He is equipping us as we travel this life together as a team bonded together by His truth and love. No longer will we be bitten or rattled with, as we peddle our way in this elaborate kingdom of harvesting! Strength is pouring in. Power is ignited. And Jesus reigns!

We have so much to be thankful for. We will be the force that oversees the kingdom, keeps it in peace, love, joy, and righteousness. We have power in the Spirit. I just heard

The Still Small Voice

while writing, "Submit to it and you will walk uprightly. Bow to it and the enemy will suffer."

"Lord,

"Triumph over us, strengthen us, increase in power, bestow us with more gifts, discernment, knowledge, wisdom, and love. Bless me, oh Lord, my coming and going. For I am the head and not the tail!

"Keep our faith alive and our marriage from ruins. Retain us in Your palm, and robe us with righteousness, honor, and integrity. Clothe us with power from on high. Kiss us with lips of sweet oil (Your words). Fasten us together with You and preserve us from the snares. Lead us with fruit bearing seeds, and encompass us with divine protection. Lift us up to soar on eagle's wings!

"Then send us to the world of unrighteousness. Let us clothe them with the truth of Your loving righteousness. Transport us the useful eternal gifts. Link us together with fearless boldness and insurmountable gallantry. Never leave us or forsake us. Formulate unprecedented paths ahead of us. Pave the way of golden streets. Empower us to deliver the light of the world. Amen (revealed from my spirit within me!)"

Your willing daughter,

Stephanie

The Still Small Voice

"And we know that in all things God works for the good of those who love Him, who have been called according to His purpose."

—Romans 8:28 NIV

Thirty-One

I Am The Fruit

A day of complete rest was in order for me. The morning dawned ... sunshine! I awoke, surprising even myself by saying, "Lord, let's spend the day together!"

I had to tackle organizing my home office and I was in complete "overwhelmed mode." So, I prayed to the Lord to help me with this. Wow! It was so smooth, quick, and actually fun! This was a joint effort and such a pleasurable one. I want to commit all my tasks to Him and learn to commune with the Master of all tasks!

As I was drawn into my bedroom, I gazed at my bedspread. A thought came to me and I considered changing it for a newer style. Immediately I was reminded that I liked classic and sophisticated styles. I was drawn to glance at the headboard and the side tables and the pictures above them, taking note that they were all in the same color scheme. Then, as if someone took my head and gently turned it completely left, I was staring at my mirrored dresser. I noticed there was not much color (other than neutrals) there also. As I continued turning, I saw the decorative luggage nearby in beautiful

shades of orange. "I really love orange," flowed from my mouth with delight! Hmmmm ... "Why do I like orange so much now?" It seems to be the dominant color beginning to emerge throughout my house and paintings. At this very moment, the Lord took me back to my childhood and I saw that it was always my favorite color! (My current favorite color is lime green.) Interesting, I thought!

It appears as if I am going back to where I left off!

I am regressing back into my childhood when innocence, dreams, promises, paths, and the hand of God appointed me. I am returning to a time before choices. Destiny before substitutes. Direction before self-reliance. Future and a hope before clutching the wheel. Wow! This is so neat! I was all His, then I took a left turn somewhere. Now I have been brought back to the path chosen by Him, before time began. I am so awed and amazed by what He is doing in my life. He is drawing me near Him, setting my feet upon the rock and living the life He planned for me. I am returning to all the desires He had placed in my heart before any corruption. I am becoming that which He designed for me.

A Sanctified Holy Creative Spirit!

Tonight in my secret place, where Jesus and I talk, I was focused on all this writing about the revelations, changes, love, sanctification, and unveiling of who He is ... it has been all for me. But something weighed heavily upon me. I know Him, but what good does it do to keep Him all for just myself. When I write and publish the book, perhaps

only a few will value it and read it. Many may not read it at all. I felt God was asking me why I felt this way. I answered Him, "I want them to see the fruit." Just then I saw God speaking and He drew into me as He spoke. And we spoke it out together as one, saying ...

"I AM THE FRUIT!"

I saw an apple in plain view, in front of me.

I walk as the fruit of Jesus. I walk, and the Lord is inside me for all to see!

As I took a big gulp of air, the tears gently flooded my face. I bowed before my heavenly Father, touching His gentle, caressing love that flowed from His being, reaching the very core of my being. Humbled before the Lord, He didn't need to be displayed on any stage or be materialized.

The fruit He had for me—before sin became an available choice for me. When I bit into it, my future and plan took its own course, like the apple tree and Eve in the garden. The good news is:

I am now restored!

When I became a Christian, by salvation in my shower, His words spoke out of my heart, unbeknownst to me, and saved me. He came for me and reconciled me to Himself! My favorite scripture became Jeremiah 29:11-12 (NIV):

"For I know the plans I have for you," declares the Lord. "Plans to prosper you, and not to harm

you. Plans to give you hope and a future."

"Then you will call on me and come and pray to me, and I will listen to you. You will seek me and find me when you seek me with all your heart. I will be found by you," declares the Lord, "and will bring you back from captivity. I will gather you from all the nations and places where I have banished you," declares the Lord, "and will bring you back to the place from which I carried you into exile."

Funny how the Lord wanted me to also write verses 12-14! He is leading me to scripture, to His word. It all falls into place as to why He had me watch an art class on how to paint an apple yesterday! So, my first prophetic, acrylic painting will be, "I AM THE FRUIT!" With this newfound revelation, my spirit continues to define who I am.

"He lives in Me and I am the evidence of the Fruit"

"Lord, I am so humbled as I bow before You. How You love! Thank you for restoring me back to You. Lord, I love spending the day with You!"

I am the evidence of Jesus!

Stephanie

Thirty-Two

Lobster on my Plate

All my recent paintings, decorations, and accents in my home have suddenly captured my attention. They are all orange flavored!

This morning, before my feet even hit the ground, after spending time fasting with God, I felt the need to repent for allowing myself a tone of persecution toward another. My life had been going too well. Things were very good, so I had to do a check-up! I asked the Lord to reveal any iniquity in my heart and I promised Him I would deal with it. I said that reluctantly, but knew it was something I was led to pray for. I chose to humble myself to gain understanding. I was being critical of a person and persecuting him for his iniquities. I find it easy to condemn when I don't stand in mercy and love. "Oh Lord, change me and forgive me and teach me Your truth. Engulf every pore, fill every opening with Your sweet love ... with the Holy Spirit."

Later this morning, I sketched a lobster on a plate, wanting it to be mine. I envisioned a ramekin of melted butter next to the lobster. I sent the picture and message off to a friend to preview. I thought it may be for her. I sent it as a text with the caption, "Lobster on MY Plate." However, when I wrote it, I saw other words in front of it. The Lord wrote, "The moment before..." I thought that was cute, funny, and endearingly appropriate. As I wondered where this fascination of sea creatures fell into my life with a desire to paint them, my Father was about to reveal His splendid love through them.

I set it aside and off to my treadmill I went. I opened my book, *Father's Embrace* by Jack Frost. I quickly became absorbed with the Holy Spirit as He began to minister to me. I was given pictures of scorned and hurt people I knew in my life. Some with deep buried pain, others having knowledge of their own behavior, inhabited by their own father's sin. I believe I had a great earthly father, but gave permission to go to the depths of my heart for any related actions that I may have with my heavenly Father, that didn't line up with the Word.

I didn't think there were any issues, but I heard the word "distant" in my spirit. Yes, it was true. I had always felt a certain distance from my natural father. Entering teen years changed my view of males, and I became distant. As I write this, revelation is coming forth. I thought my dad was distant but the Spirit just informed me that I was the one who withdrew emotionally. Just like I did with my heavenly Father, hid my face and regressed. I didn't have an affectionate relationship with my father. The words, "I love you," never rang clear. I knew I was my father's daughter, and I knew he was pleased with me. I was "the good one ... the favorite one," he would say. Both of my parents are now living in eternity, citizens of heaven in the Kingdom of God. Though I miss them, I am rejoicing in their eternal abundance. My heart sinks at the loss and how I would be more willing to share a nurtured and mature relationship with them. I yearn for them and miss my dad's protection, wisdom, covering, and love.

I am able to recognize the very things I missed most from my father, God had for me. This afternoon, I know He adopted me and I am not fatherless. I am embellished with His grace. I humbly repent for looking mistakenly upon the Lord through my circumstances. He healed me and restored me to a Father's love, and I am His. Oh, happy days!

I began to sing to the Lord as I walked. The words were sweet to the Lord's ears as He had me hear it as it goes up to heaven's choir. And the sound that came back to me told me how it pleased Him! He filled me with such joy! I declared who I was in Christ, joyfully, out loud. I was restored instantly and immediately with my heavenly Father. There was no longer distance between us, no gap! We unite and the sound is so sweet. The whole room was filled with heaven's scent of beauty, as I sang out to the Lord of His great love! I am restored and not forgotten. I filtered what I had with my dad, with my Father. It wasn't

true. He longs for me, adores me, and loves me just as I am! He cares so deeply for me. I am His favorite one!

I went back downstairs and was taken to the view of my sketch. Again I heard, "The moment before... ."

The moment before, I didn't know. The next moment I was immersed in His love and mercy (like a lobster swimming in sweet butter, not knowing what lies ahead)!

The painting is now labeled, **"The Moment Before"** and the revelation writing is: **"The moment before the transfer of new found love ... and you drown in it!"**

Today, let the love of God consume your every pore. Allow His blood to cover you. Ask Him to restore you. When He knew you and created you, He didn't make a mistake. He is perfect in all His ways to come. He wants His children. Come forth and come boldly. He awaits you with open arms, ready to embrace you today.

"Lord, how I love You. I pray that everyone who reads this story gets drenched by Your love. Amen."

Captivated by His love,

Stephanie

---

*"The LORD will fulfill [His purpose} for me;
Your love, O LORD, endures forever—do not
abandon the works of Your hands."*

—Psalm 138:8 NIV

Thirty-Three

The Gem of the Sea

I have been drawn to paintings of crabs for quite some time. Until this moment, I didn't know why!

I saw a vision of me painting a piece of a crab's shell, a crab which I will affectionately call him, Crabby! The shell was a beautiful turquoise color. It looked like a gem! It was precise and vivid. I asked the Lord, "What is it with this crab?" He showed me again the chunk of turquoise shell and said, "It's the Gem of the Sea!"

I stood still for a moment. Then He expanded the vision within my spirit. The true gems of the treasure are found on the bottom of the ocean! "Whoa," I said! "Really?"

Then I heard, "Well, don't crabs walk on the bottom of the ocean?"

"Yep-per," I said!

Like the treasure chest filled with gems, you have to dive down deeper into the ocean, past all the fish and sea

critters, and sharks in order to see and receive the precious gems He has stored up for you. They are waiting for you to discover and seize!

As I am writing this, a new revelation just caught me by surprise. Just like the coin that was found in the fish's mouth ... hidden! God's treasure chest for me was hidden on the bottom of the ocean! I had to float, swim, waddle, dive, and even sink at times through adversities, trials, and transformations, to have my eyes opened to the truth. But most importantly, I had to get out of the boat! Now I can enjoy the rewards.

During a special guest speaking at our church about two years ago, the Lord showed me something that stuck with me. Now I have experienced the significance of that.

I was in a boat in the ocean. I heard a voice say, "Get out. Get out of the boat." So I did and saw myself floating.

He said, "Dive down." So I did and saw all the little fishies. Most were cute and in tropical colors. It was delightful. Then I heard, "Go further." So I swam a little deeper. The fish changed to larger ones, and were still friendly. Then I went to another level where they were big!

I heard, "Keep going." So I dove really deep and saw all the dangerous sharks around me. I felt the danger and needed caution and wisdom to survive. I even saw huge whales that could swallow me up quickly. I got past them and it became all dark around me. I didn't understand where I was or why.

I heard distinctly, "Dive deeper. Keep going and look." I obeyed, and all of a sudden the water was clear and beautiful and I could see the bottom which had beautiful, soft white sand. There, what came into view was a treasure chest. It was old-fashioned looking and the lid was wide opened for me as I approached it!

To my astonishment, I saw an overflowing chest full of beautiful, sparkling, gorgeous jewels. There were pearls, gems, diamonds, gold, silver, necklaces, bracelets, and more!

I believe all my pruning, trimming, replanting, uprooting, and fertilizing has come to a point where I can now have the privilege of seeing the tree bear much fruit!

The painting is labeled, "Crabby." The revelation writing is: "The Gem of the Sea. You have to dive deep to receive the precious gems He has stored up for you. They are waiting for you to discover and seize!"

In Adoration,

Stephanie

The Still Small Voice

"These things God has revealed
to us through the Spirit.
For the Spirit searches everything,
even the depths of God."

—1 Corinthians 2:10 ESV

Thirty-Four

Just Follow Me!

I received an invitation to attend a Warrior Princess conference and overly tired, I thought for a second about not attending. My husband told me to pray about it.

I did ... and heard, "Give it away."

My spirit let me know that going to this conference wasn't about me! It wasn't about an opportunity for me to be filled up this time. Often when a conference comes up, I think about me and what I can get out of it. But it was about someone else this time. To my surprise, I was appointed to love, bear witness, and be still. Praying in my secret place gave allowance for a very loving, gentle impartation by my Father. No explanation was given, faith had empowered me to trust and obey Him.

My friend picked me up at my home and we drove off to the church. We prayed together before entering the church. The sanctuary was filled with women and the service was in overflow and there were not enough tables set up! My girlfriend sought out the leaders and two minutes later we were sitting at the front behind a newly set up table! As we took ownership of this table, a gentleman came over and said he needed to move our table over to make space to add yet another table. So, reluctantly I moved to the next table which was further away from the vicinity of the speaker. A women began finger counting the seating capacity around our table, and selfishly I told her there would be a larger table over yonder in a moment. She gathered her guests and shuttled them quickly around the same table. We crammed in together, all nine of us!

As worship began, I fell right into it. It was so sweet with His presence. I camped out there. I leaned over to my friend as we stood with our hands and hearts raised and I whispered in her ear: "There is something going on at our table and we need to pray over it."

She said, "Okay," with a trusting heart and no knowledge. There were no introductions, and it struck me as strange that there was none of the "usual" conversation around our table. After all, I am the social one! They were younger girls and gave me the impression they were individually set apart.

The Spirit began to stir me. As we worshipped and entered deeper, His presence draped around me with immeasurable love. We had stepped away from our table during worship to be in a secret place with Him. When I returned to sit back down after the music ceased, the Spirit made me look at their stomach area. He told me in the Spirit that they were

all pregnant! I gently, with discretion, hugged my friend in joy and revealed the revelation I received. She exclaimed, "Oh really!" So we prayed silently for them with joy in our hearts.

Lunch arrived at all the tables. I didn't know how to approach this and I didn't want to be intrusive. I got a check in my spirit that I had not earned their friendship or the right to inquire. So, I prayed over this and then spoke. I said, "Hello. Do ya'll know each other?"

One of the young girls replied, "Yes, we do! We are pregnant and all live together at _____."

"Oh," I said, "Okay." She had offered this information openly with a kindness that was inviting.

"So what now God?" I asked.

He didn't answer, so I just ate my lunch!

We had a few more speakers and they played more worship music inbetween. By day's end, I was overwhelmed in the full presence of the Lord. Tears rolled down my face as we sang about how beautiful He is ... Yahweh. I wanted to invite the women who brought these girls here, to visit our church. I gave her a card, but it was quite a distance for them to drive. I knew deep down that I would see them again, although I had only a moment of contact.

As the conference dismissed, I was surprised to hear, "Sit down!"

We responded as if a chief had just spoken! I whispered to my friend, "Perhaps you better speak to their chaperone first for her approval."

She looked at me, and said, "I already did!"

I giggled inside. She shared the words the Lord had for them and I just burst into tears. It was as if my heart jumped out of me. I tried to hold back and even swung my entire hand and covered my mouth. I think now, that I cried in the Spirit (a first for me) because no one even noticed. She had verbalized what the Lord had also revealed to me by Spirit!

I was going to ask to pray over them with permission from their chaperone, but my friend beat me to the punch! The Lord gave both of us the same message and we never consulted with each other—not a single word, not a knowing look to one another. The new information I heard was a life desire of my friend to have a home for unwed pregnant mothers. I have a heart's desire to finance His appointed kingdom purposes as He leads me. Now that's a divine sisterhood!

Although my heart grieved for their circumstances, the Lord put on my heart to pray over them. I gently asked for permission from these precious ones and from their chaperone. They all leaped forward with great expectation across the round table! They squeezed together. The first question He had me ask was if they were all saved? They were! Oh how the sweet Lord just placed His hand upon their lives with immense love! I know it was not me speaking or feeling, but the Holy Spirit pouring Himself out upon them. This came to me as a surprise also! He told them who they

are in Christ. He pulled Himself from the inside of them and wrapped around them like a cloak of liquid love.

But the best was yet to come! As we stood up to leave, each one of them rushed into my arms and shed their pain, and deepest pains of grief. They opened with endearing trust to a total stranger and brought forth confessions of truth bearing, releasing their deepest confessions to my spirit within. As I am writing this, that beautiful moment is as clear as when it happened and I am overwhelmed by the love He has for them. I was filled completely with the Holy Spirit and felt Him breathe on them. The first girl spoke of her situation of adoption and I felt like my insides burst. She then buried her head into my shoulder without hesitation. The Lord whispered into her ear as I held her close with one hand on her precious head and the other around her as she released herself in Him.

The next pulled me into her after her confession and wept profusely in my arms. They next gave her one liner also, and God gave her the permission to giggle and laugh in her life, for it was His gift from Him. The next shivered with hurt and shame, but God raised her to a height of honor and love. The next spoke and I asked her age. I repeated it back to her as grief gripped my heart with wrenching pain. Tears just streamed down my face. She grabbed my heart through her unspeakable situation. I could feel everything she was feeling at that very moment without uttering another word. The Lord let her know how valuable she was to Him, and how worthy. They were so beautiful, highly valued, worthy, cherished, priceless, gorgeous women in Christ. It was as

if they wanted to talk to Jesus Himself. I listened and God uncovered the depth of their heart and He healed them. For it was not I who stood before them, but Christ in the flesh. They actually touched the very One who crafted them. It was as if I was watching this unleash as I saw Jesus manifest in front of me. I saw Him ahead of me in a white gown, embracing His daughters with His pure heart.

I will personally treasure this divine time in my heart as one of the most intimate moments in my life.

We received an open invitation from the chaperone to come visit them. As they departed, it was clear we had bonded in an instant through the loving arms of Jesus.

Lord, thank You for placing me in Your timing, at Your table! Your love endures even to the lowly at heart. You took their pain to Calvary and set them free. I thank You that I followed you to the cross today. I lay myself down once again on the altar and say, I am all Yours. Use me to Your will.

I am humbly grateful for the invitation to this event to testify of the love of God. Now I know for the next time … I don't need to know the "Why," just the "I will."

"God, bless these six girls and lead them into all truth for they are the inheritance and beloved children of the kingdom. Amen."

Following You,

Thirty-Five

He Reigns

The Lord showed me that my husband is like "A Gallant Warrior Horse," who is snorting and pawing at the ground with his hooves, ambitiously ready to get out of the gate and go into the future. But the Lord is holding his reigns. It is God holding him back. He said: "I haven't given him the tools yet!"

The Lord leads me into the insight through vision, and this is what He showed me:

My husband desperately wants to leave the gate, and he is enclosed behind the rail along with all the other race horses on the track. As he aggressively anticipates, with the force of strength, the gate opens! Off they go, running as fast as they can, but he slips and falls in the first turn. As he tumbles to the ground of the track, he looks back at the starting gate (where I am) and smiles valiantly. He thinks the race is over. But I look around and see the other horses still running the race. I cheer him on yelling through my

cupped hands, "Get up! Keep going! The race isn't over yet ... you can do it!"

"It's not over until you cross the finish line," God says, "Go for the goal!"

My husband smiles and grins at me with loving eyes. And the Lord says to him, "You walk in mighty, powerful integrity and do not compromise the worthy treasures I have instilled in you. It is important for you, My beloved son, to know that no two men are alike. I made you unique for a very high calling. So keep your eyes on Me and the finish line, and run that race for Me, run well." (Says the Lord.)

He is being trained and in his zeal wants to go out before he is ready!

My husband diligently seeks the will of His Father. He is so hungry for God—ravishing, like a courageous warrior horse in the gate, ready and willing to burst through! He keeps his son safe, in protection mode, until it is the appointed time. But patience is not on the menu today, ravishing hunger to run the race is! So today the Lord says, "Son, wait upon Me for the great bell to go off. For only I know when that time will be."

Then God shows me His hands upon the reigns and says, "Whoa!"

We both want to be unleashed, but we're not fully equipped yet! Oh, this is so good! As I share the unveiling

The Still Small Voice

picture ... vision, revelation, and words of God ... my husband is full, peaceful, and very happy!

He will wait upon the Lord's command in complete obedience, with absolute trust in and love for his Father.

"Lord,

"You have me tearing up again, even though I try to hold back my tears. Hearing Your loving words as I type completes my heart ... to see the love the Father has for His son, my husband. How You love him. OH, how You love him so dearly."

In adoration for the both of you, my dearest loves,

Stephanie

The Still Small Voice

"May you experience
the love of Christ, though it is
so great you will never fully
understand it. Then you
will be filled with the fullness
of life and power
that comes from God."

—Ephesians 3:19 NLT

Thirty-Six

His Courts

I just got to the final place ... He told me, "It is in His courts!" I am so elated at the moment, I'm overwhelmed in JOY!

The prophetic word I received on Saturday already came to be! My burning question is:

"When Lord? When and where?"

He showed me that it's not a geographical place. It's dwelling in the house of the Lord.

"It's where I am," He says.

"Constant and never ending ..."
(I just heard while typing).

"Blessed are those You choose and bring near to live in Your courts! We are filled with the good things of Your house, of Your Holy temple."

Psalm 65:4

The Still Small Voice

Hey ... "I ARRIVED!"

I am going to shout it on the mountain!

"I have arrived!"

I have been waiting for this my whole life. I have finally entered into the place I was born for! It's the Holy place where He is. All the training, trials, conforming, obeying, listening, thirsting, I am now here! Oh, and it is so beautiful. I no longer live by my flesh, but by the mighty hand of God Himself. Led by the Spirit, communing as one. Soaring in jubilee in the third heaven! Wow!

It is not a time for humbling, but a time of exaggerated euphoric satisfaction in a place I have never been before. In His courts! Staying and not tumbling. Standing and not trembling. Knowing and never fearing. Joyful and not worried. Full and overflowing, not empty and wandering. Still and peaceful, not anxious. Grateful and exemplifying humility. Justified and not boastful. Patiently in love, compassionate for others and giving, and not judging or withholding. Complete and not broken. Fed and fully satisfied and not hungry for the world. Sharing Him and not self-reliant, nor selfish. I have a new heart after love, not after anything else!

As I write this, my eyes fill with tears at the marvelous ways God has conformed me. How much He loves me and how gracious He is to us. I am overflowing in the precious mercy my Father has—not only for me, but how He wants

to give it to all of us. It hurts and pains my heart that not everyone comes to the well to drink of His love.

"If there is a way that I can direct Your children, Lord, please use me to do that. There is life here. Nowhere else can even a drop be found that compares to the majestic love of You. Teach us, show us, send more, and let me give it away Lord.

"Father, I love and adore You beyond words. They will know us by the Father's love. Here, in Your courts, I am struck by the vastness of Your love. Please, Lord, please, show me how to give it to others."

I hear, "Draw them to me," says the Lord, "and I will feed them."

"Anything Lord, anything You tell me to say or do, I will obey. Here I am ..."

In Your courts,

Stephanie

The Still Small Voice

"How lovely is Your tabernacle,
O LORD of hosts!
My soul longs, yes, even faints
For the courts of the LORD;
My heart and my flesh cry out for
the living God."
—Psalms 84:1-2 NKJV

Thirty-Seven

Gotcha'

The neatest thing happened to me last night. I caught what was going on in my spirit while I slept! I awoke during the time God was communicating with my spirit! I surprised God by awakening ... or so I thought ... then I just had to giggle, thinking that somehow I thought I gotten one over on God. Ha! Don't you think He planned that for me? Of course He did! He had such delight in me as He grinned and chuckled at my childlike adoration and playfulness with Him!

I have found that no matter how you try to describe Jesus, He is so marvelous that nothing can capture the essence of the true reality of Who and What He is. Such as a color you see—like you have never seen before and can't describe it because it doesn't exist in your frame of reference and you have no vocabulary developed enough to describe what you experience when you see it. The same thing happens with revelations, prophetic words, dreams, feelings, feathers, angels, and miracles.

They are from the supernatural realm and beyond our capacity to comprehend or contain.

So having said that, I will attempt to share my incredible experience. I awoke with such an incredible warmth, delight, and awesome fascination of what heaven looks like! He had my spirit there. I **know** I was there and it was so beautiful. I literally have no words to describe it. It was as if I had to tell people how incredible it was and what to expect. It was beyond comprehension in its beauty. Not only visually, but in the place of God's presence it was even more stunning. I just breathed in His goodness and was in jubilee of delight and fascination. I thought I was awake, but now I am still not sure! I knew I had to tell my husband for fear I wouldn't remember when I awoke in the morning. The Lord revealed to me that, as I do His will and purpose as He has called me to, my reward in heaven awaits me. That it is all worth it.

The comfort of not doing it for earthly reward or credit was fulfilling. What is set before me on earth is easy to endure because it is just so incredibly worth it all. My mind lingers on the scripture that tells how He rewards those who diligently seek Him.

I am tearing up as I am touched by His love and level of gentleness. It is overwhelming that lil' ole' me has been chosen by Him. I have undoubtedly laid down my life for Him and He brings me to another level, elevating us to an unseen realm where we can see in the Spirit. He welcomes us into the drafted army. I am believing all He has for us, just because I have faith big enough. He is setting us apart for His glory as He takes us into transition for the great realignment of His takeover. All of me has been shaken and will be set upon a new foundation—His tabernacle of final glory, re-establishing His rightful place at the altar. The pieces were adding up. We tried to reason, convince, and rationalize our thoughts and circumstances that were disturbing to us. But I believe now, He has brought His Great Commission into alignment.

What we had believed before, had now surfaced as direction from the Lord. Endorsing absolute power to be His prophet hinges on the yielding power to the God we are to believe. (I just typed the first letter I heard and then He completed it all!)

"Lord, you know we love You unconditionally and we are Your loving children. You find favor in us and we obey out of love for You. Please protect us as we follow your directions. Grant us favor and provision to accomplish all you have for us. We adopt You! The time has come to release us into our destiny. We will move on not from our doing, but of Your doing."

"Lord, remove the obstacles that hinder us to our sinking. We establish new borders and spread out our tents in the new places. Please prune all that is adolescent, Lord. We are risk-takers for the kingdom and we have an inspiration to aspire! There is no blueprint in these uncharted waters. Unleash all the powers to guide us upon the pathway to your specific plan."

God had been nudging us for the past several months. But now we glorify the Lord in it. We know His mighty hand was always upon us, giving us a relational habitat to dwell in. His courts!

"Lord, Your majestic Being has taken me to the high place. I am humbled and ever so grateful for the time You have invested in me and never letting me go. I feel I have arrived to that finer place ... a place I have waited for and searched for my whole life. I no longer run after the things of the world. I truly have no interest in them, but the true jewels set before me, I have tasted and seen. Those are the everlasting treasures. They are filled with precious stones, bundles of joy, abounding with angelic angels, laughter, true happiness, peace, and ... "

"It is where I AM," the Lord said.

Now I can openly and freely say, 'It is where I am!"

"Can we truly have this?" I asked Him.

"Yes and yes!" He said.

As your empowered soldiers, we establish the new season with alignment and boldness, strengthened with more operational power at an accelerated rate!

I received a turning point and my husband felt he received a tipping point in his spirit. We can justly say, the tables have turned! Our journey continues as God's chosen ones. We go willingly, lovingly, and submissively.

We go for the sake of the Lord who calls us His beloved children.

We are being expanded by pressure. Now I know why I was to buy the condensed orange strainer I saw while shopping for luggage for our trip to Cabo San Lucas to attend Lance Wallnau's "Destiny Dream Weekend" with his tribe! We are in a colander and He is gently pressing us into fine wine through the seive! It's the "Purification."

"Lord, we have enrolled to a new dimension. I sensed we instantaneously crossed over a threshold into new territory, one we haven't seen before. We are being trained up! And with this acknowledgement, I anticipate colossal advancement from this day forward. Our steps have clearly been ordered by You, therefore, I believe the resounding voice will guide us into our true callings very soon. Patiently we waited, and patiently You gave."

Devoted forever,

Stephanie

The Still Small Voice

"He has set the compass and given us directions for the destiny of His house."

—Stephanie M. Lumbia

Thirty-Eight

Keys to The Kingdom

I am still in awe of what happened yesterday as we received a Mantle. I heard the Sheckles chime and my husband felt the enormous weight of the chest! In fact, I was just in our kitchen and expressed to my husband how significant this gift was that was given to us unexpectedly by a couple.

I began by saying , "We have crossed over into the," and the Holy Spirit spoke, "The threshold."

He turned my eyes to where the kitchen met the dinette area. I looked directly to the floor. I was standing inside the threshold!

"Lord, what a way you express Yourself so I can understand! How beautiful … and, I think, artistic! Wow! What has truly happened will unfold in the days to come.

I have no idea what "The Mantle" holds. Other than I have always declared that we would (my husband and I) be able to give financially—and give big—to the enlargement of the

kingdom across the world. We will be giving in lots of ways. But, especially we desire to be able to provide funding to advance the needs of leaders to accomplish what God has set out to do. The level of importance is measured by God, not by me. Places to touch are His domain, not mine. In which ways to touch or give are His decisions, not ours. If we do our part and obey Him, He will clearly tell us.

"Lord, I press into You to mobilize us and put us on the right paths. Guide us into all truth and protect us. Use us, oh Lord and we humbly say, 'I am Yours through and through.' Let us not stumble, let us not stray, but be complete in the knowledge to the Righteous One who sits on the right side of Christ Almighty, as your humble servants. (This is what I just heard.) Amen."

Lord, I trust You ...

Stephanie

"Each one must give as he has decided in his heart, not reluctantly or under compulsion, for God loves a cheerful giver."

—2 Corinthians 9:7 ESV

Thirty-Nine

Mirror, Mirror On The Wall

As I walked on my treadmill at home, I was brought to full humility, meditating upon the kindness of God!

I was full of frustration concerning two family members whom I love dearly. They are saved, but have a different understanding than we have come to experience. My husband and I desire to communicate and fellowship with them on some spiritual level. We would like to share living in His kingdom and not living by worldly standards and thinking. I am seeking clarity, and I need the voice of the Lord to speak loudly to me ... at this given moment!

I asked my Father with sincerity and a troublesome heart,

"When will they get it?"

"When will they be sold out for You? Your love is above all, it is true and incredible! Your ways are higher than ours and is so grand! All that You have, is for us. It's an incredible life in You."

"In fact, when will they all (the world) get it?"

He spoke through my spirit and I posed this question with meekness: "How God? How do You want me to lie down for them?"

He answered, "In undying love, like the cross." He showed me the wooden cross in all its majestic sanctification.

He replied to me by showing me a lake with plenty of rippling water and said, "Mirror, Mirror." I didn't get it at first. Then the water separated from the middle out and turned into this smoothness that represented a glass-like finish. I quickly withdrew and kept repeating the words from His conviction, "I know, I know, I'm so sorry."

Peering back at me from the lake was the reflection of myself! I was being gently reminded of my own doubts and unbelief as a new creature, one in which He gently reminds me that took much patience to overcome. Yes, myself! I'm to have the same mercy of love for consideration with others that was so graciously given to me by my Father. I was acknowledging my own gestation of my growth from infancy until now.

I took in a deep breath and exhaled as I heard in my spirit the word, "disciple." Even His closest ones (the original twelve disciples) had to be "discipled" by the "discipler." For He even calls me, "a disciple of Christ!" Whoa!

For I too, am not without fault, and I am in need of being discipled. Perhaps this is a lesson in humility to meet people

right where they are in Christ. For it is He who will finish the good works in us. I quickly repented with a sorrowful heart as the light shined back to me, on the lake of living waters. I fell on my knees, weeping.

Just to increase me more, He didn't give up on me just yet. He kept right on with another vision. Just when I didn't think I could be humbled any further! He showed me a mirror on a table stand. I could see it was Jesus looking into the mirror at an angle. Then the Lord spoke to me and said, "Who do you see when you look in the mirror?"

He placed me in the vision, sitting in front of the mirror. I noticed there was not a reflection of me in the mirror, but His. Because it is He who sees and is in me. My reflection is Him—who people see—and it's who He sees! Wow!

I mirror Jesus!

Lord, this is truly humbling to the core. I will forever remember this moment You shared with me. I want to always reflect who You are. Humble me more to Thy ways, Lord.

Thank You for revealing Jesus in me! I love Your teachings dearly.

Reflecting You,

Stephanie

The Still Small Voice

"Now we see but a poor reflection as in a mirror; then we shall see face to face. Now I know in part; then I shall know fully, even as I am fully known."

—1 Corinthians 13:12 NIV

Forty

Stop, Sit, and Pray

I have a full plate in task management! I am juggling writing and art. The guilt over spending the majority of my time, to center my focus on this, is overwhelming me. I feel I should be working and achieving like the rest of the world, and in the evening, be with my husband. So, when is there time to write and create art without feeling the tug of robbing anyone's time? I feel kind of self-centered and a little selfish. This has become a big project now and the time demand is even higher. I know He is calling me to do this. I need balance and an answer.

I generously submitted this to my Father and received His loving answer in the evening. He gave me very specific hours to set aside daily to write and to paint. That was easy enough! Going ahead a few days, I must admit, I have not completely worked inside this time frame, but something more importantly emerged. All the guilt, selfishness, anxiety, stress, and every other negative feeling thrown

my way about taking time out to do God's work within my day left me! He healed me from self-condemnation. This is a recognition of self-striving and God's glorious mercy stepping in with an invitation to be released from all of that stuff. This is God. Whatever He has called us to do is light and easy, because it is accomplished in His strength, not in the might of personal striving and growing ever-so-weary beneath the weight. I am resting in His perfect timing that He established, so it brings peace and conviction with freedom to do the Father's work! His yoke is light and His burden is easy! I am content as I relish in my tasks! I did not even have to enforce this within the household. It came with ease, because it was His will.

"Lord, I know you are teaching me to reach out to you. Forgive me for striving on my own and making peace with myself. I see clearly that it was I, creating the stress and that You are permitting me to enjoy my life. I love what I am doing and thank You for renewing my mind. This place is so incredible as You draw me back to You! It really causes the old self to shed. You want us happy! Sometimes we don't permit ourselves to be that. I fully enjoy my art and writing, but felt guilt over the time commitment, causing strife and anxiety that consumed valuable time. You drew me into You for the Sabbath rest, keeping on with the art and writing, embellished with increased pleasure! How beautiful You are!"

I thought since the art and writing went well, I could ask boldy for a time to go to the gym too! Guess what? You guessed it, He gave me a time for that too! 7:00 AM. It makes perfect sense with the continuation of time He gave me to schedule for writing: 8:00 AM - 3:00 PM!!

I didn't fully understand that God was interested in the small things. But He is. He even gave me an eating plan with times! Sometimes we put aside the very essence of His precise measure of order for our own essential scheduling. We push and stretch our days to accomplish all that we would like to do instead of what He is ordering to do.

Yes, He cares and knows what is best for us. All along, the enemy was throwing out condemnation and guilt to me, telling me that I wasn't disciplined enough to do the things God called me to do, or that if I did them, I wasn't being a good wife, mother, or business owner. When I brought this to God, He told me, "You are a great planner. I love you and will always be with you."

I think I'll stick with Gods' plan!

Redeemed,

Stephanie

The Still Small Voice

"But I trust in you, O Lord;
I say, 'You are my God.'
My times are in Your hand;
rescue me from the hand of my
enemies and from my persecutors!"

—Psalm 31:14-15 ESV

Forty-One

A Fresh Revelation

I received this scripture today from the Father: *"So we are Christ's ambassadors, God making His appeal as it were through us. We (as Christ's personal representatives) beg you for His sake to lay hold of the divine favor (now offered you) and be reconciled to God"* (2 Corinthians 5:20, AMP).

The Lord breathed on me!

His new encounter with us in this shift is not coming through our intelligence—not through our thinking. It is not even being poured in or poured down. It is coming to us through the wind!

I believe the word I received is this:

We are having a fresh new wind breathed on us through the battle to realign us to Christ.

The Lord just gave me this revelation about what He is doing. This is incredible! Yes, we are in a battle, but He is using it to make all things new again. His mighty wind flows

all between us, and He breathes new life in us. We will be like new. He is realigning us back to Him, but in a new way. It is through His divine breath.

We will not be able to stand in "the now" like we used to. He is in charge of the mighty army, and His breath aligns us to heaven's ways.

I believe the Lord is purging the old leaven from your life, that you may be fresh dough (See 1 Corinthians 5:6).

Whoa! For the past two months I have been getting quite a download. I have been receiving confirmation through people, TV, conferences, mailings, and pastors. I have seen what He is doing in the Spirit. My eyes seem to have been shifted. When I look back the past month or so, I see He gave me insight, but realize that I didn't have the mature understanding.

Then He personally took me through the process (or journey) with Him. So now when I look back, I am ecstatic about what He has done! It is incredible! The euphoric, over-the top, exhilarating joy of capturing the mystery revealed ... it is indescribable! When this happens this way, there is such an overwhelming awe at His love and greatness. He has begun something new in me.

Foreseeing perhaps? Prophesying maybe? I'm not sure exactly, but I don't need to categorize it. ***I Just know it is God and He sets me on fire!*** I am sitting quietly in awe, but internally I am jumping ecstatically with elation!

We all have so much to be thankful for. He is doing so much for us, but you have to look with your spiritual eyes and not your natural eyes in order to see it! It's time for Christians to arise and take note. This is giving us the opportunity to rejoice in the Lord and boast in what He is doing! This is for all of us. He is Commander of the army and we trust what He is doing. Wow! Wake up and seek the Lord. Join in the magnificent works of the Lord. He is taking back His kingdom on earth! Don't let the parade pass you by. Rejoice!

Territory outside the walls of the church needs to be seized. He is not only calling up His saints, but purifying the loaves to glorify Himself. Arise, oh Lord, arise! Redefine what Christianity is.

This just arose out of my spirit, "I want a worldwide ministry." I stand in agreement with this!

"Thank you, Lord, for this glorious time. You have given me Spiritual eyes to see in your kingdom realm! Amen."

With exuberant excitement and joy,

Stephanie

The Still Small Voice

"These are the things God has revealed to us by his Spirit. The Spirit searches all things, even the deep things of God."

—1 Corinthians 2:10 NIV

Forty-Two

His Name Above All Names

"Today is the day the Lord hath made. Rejoice and be glad in it!"

A beautiful day it shall be. Rejoice and be glad in it! Claim it, as if it already is! This is a day of jubilee! Relish in Him today! My flesh always has a different agenda than God's, but He will make all things work together for my good. Always. I need to be led. "I am not the leader. I must not disregard and dismiss the teacher."

I think right now, a lot us have been stirred, and as He raises the bar, we step into an unfamiliar and uncomfortable climate. Because He is strategically placing us, much of what we are experiencing is a newness from the stale way of doing things. There is a fresh wind blowing in every direction and it will touch everyone. We will be directed by our Father, led into unfamiliar territories. "Foreign," will be our gateway into new, stable land in this awakening! The old ways of thinking are not acceptable or profitable in this

new season. The fermented dough is no more. The leaven (sin) must go. We must be cleaned up. Purification unto Him only.

It's going to be a rough road to get to the correct path, but once on it ... aahh ... that's where the glory is! That is where I want to be.

God is serious. He is strategic as He aligns us, His saints. Greatness is arising! Hallelujah! So I pray:

"Place me, oh Lord. Show me Your face on the compass. Lead me in the way and into all truth. We go ahead of the opposition and take back what was stolen. When they come in darkness, we do not need to fear. We know that this territory is already established by and into the kingdom. You are a mighty fortress. You never falter or fail. Show us Your glory in this hour. Amen."

Awakened,

Stephanie

Forty-Three

The Holy of Holies

For the past two days, the Lord has had me mostly at home, luring me into my bathroom. It is my secret place! (Don't worry, I have a big bathroom!)

Wow, I just caught hold of the imagine God wanted to show me. This is huge! We have to know what's happening in the spirit. We are in a paradigm shift. This was confirmed to me on a God channel this morning. I couldn't label it, but I received confirmation when the Lord wanted me to turn the channel on. That's how God speaks to me, in everyday avenues!

When Peter stepped out of the boat in faith, he was fine until he began to think based on his old patterns. He quickly discovered that old thinking will cause you to fail, to sink. You cannot go forth with your old thinking. What worked in the old will not work in the new. It's not just about the Lord shaking all that can be shaken anymore. A shift has taken the lead role! We are stepping into uncharted waters

in the vast ocean. We have never been there before. Once you step into the shift, all things become new. You can't use what you knew before. This is clear to us as we read Luke and Matthew.

Even though some may be tempted to stay where it is safe and comfortable, we (my husband and I) have chosen to go at any cost. We won't be stuck in the duck stage! Something is on the verge of breaking through in vast proportion that will move the entire nation! I choose to commit and obey His path set before me. We need His strength to operate in this new place ahead of us. I don't want to miss the boat, I will be aboard! It is so exciting for all of us! Oh, what an incredible time we have been engaged in!

I got this fresh revelation this morning shortly after, an aquaintence called me in excitement, so I shared that download from heaven that had engulfed me. A friend questioned my whereabouts. But I realized that whatever words I spoke to my friend, she couldn't transfer them into the slot of her level of understanding. "Why?" I asked the Lord. The answer was revealed to me by my inner spirit. "Because she would fit it into her current mindset." No matter what I said, it would be misconstrued in translation, resulting in absolute tethering. There was no appropriate answer. Whatever I said would mingle with her old thoughts to fit in, like a puzzle piece, adjusting to fit in the space to connect for her understanding. Lost in translation perhaps, or lost in space! But I spoke it out of the new place I had already entered into spiritually.

The Still Small Voice

You can't put God in a bucket!

See, once you hit the tipping point, you can't go back. Only forward. You can't fit the new thinking and the new ways in the old box anymore. We may try to rationalize and make things fit into our little spaces, but it won't fit in that slot, because it's something that is fresh. It has been spoken in the new, as in the shift and turn that was pre-ordained, and we just had the privilege to enter in!

> *"And it occurred that on the eighth day, when they came to circumcise the child, they were intending to call him Zachariah after his father, But his mother answered, Not so! But he shall be called John."*
>
> *Luke 1:59*

This was the preceding word. It's about what comes after!

Oh Glory to God! A new name and a new day! It's what came after the first word that made all the difference! She had changed from tradition to destiny by calling in the future of her newborn son through prophetic promises in the word.

The church is the people and He is reforming it. I do not have to be contained within the four walls. Church is not about the building. God has told me I am already in His place. I am seated at the right hand of the Father in heavenly places. High above the mantle. He has me outside of the four walls to be with Him and go where He instructs.

As He previously gave me this revelation: the fourth side of the wall is opened for His rightful place—the pulpit! I don't think my friend can comprehend this without fitting that into her mind as something else. We have entered into the Holy of Holies, the third dimension.

I am so excited to have received this revelation today. The Lord is having us pick up things along the way. They are the necessary tools and treasures for our ministry and true destiny!

"Lord, I pray for a fresh awakening for all Your children. Release them to grow. Not to be confined, but rise with the eagle, and soar. Breathe on them with Holy breath. Bring them into the Glorious light of the Holy of Holies, enlarged by Your scope and not by human hands.

"You are so merciful and joyful! Draw us into Your presence and give us extraordinary sensitivity to the Holy Spirit for wisdom and truth. As we pass this journey, give our rightful inheritance and preordained destiny. Amen."

Your prized one,

Stephanie

"Oh, what a wonderful God we have! How great are His riches and wisdom and knowledge! How impossible it is for us to understand His decisions and His methods! ... For everything comes from Him; everything exists by His power and is intended for His glory. To Him be glory evermore. Amen."

—Romans 11:33-36

Forty-Four

The Master Groomer

Divine appointments have been the regular for me this past month! The Lord has put many women in my path who needed God's love bestowed upon them. This has been so humbling for me, to watch what the Lord is saying into someone's life other than my own!

We spontaneously stopped in a car maintenance repair shop. We came to price brakes, fluids, wheel rotation, and alignment ... to the best of my non-mechanic mentality! A women turned to me and said she couldn't help but to overhear our conversation and wanted to listen to more! My husband and I were having a discussion on obedience and non-tolerance to evil spirits! This is commanded in the book of Revelation. Our spiritual eyes were opening to truth as it was needed, timed by God. I love how He brings forth His words just when the perfect time is upon us. We all introduced ourselves and our conversation lasted for some time. The Lord gave me insight into her life. He shared details

with me such as; she had three cats, a desk job, boldness, and then I saw a big empty chair. I didn't know the meaning of any of this, but she sure did! She felt like what she was running after wasn't going to be obtained here and she was ready to go back to her home many states away with her cats and her mother in tow. The Lord had apparently brought boldness to her by setting up her tent elsewhere. And the chair? There was a very large chair sitting empty in her office and she wondered if she returned to her job, if they would appreciate her more now. The Lord told me that He wanted to see if she would take up His cross and follow Him. It gave her a newfound awareness and other growth. I believe He repositioned her geographically in the natural, and definitely repositioned her in the spiritual realm. This is exciting! She is returning with a new mindset. He touched her. She said she was looking for something here and I believe she truly found it! It just showed up in a completely new way she didn't expect it to. How exciting!

Here is another story: I briefly met two sisters at a conference. Then God happened to sit us together at the very next conference! We spoke once again for just a moment. She asked me for my number. I had received a call from her. The Lord had me wake her at 10:00 PM to talk to her! I apologized for not looking at the clock, but it was God who wanted to bring her peace and take the reins from her. He lifted up her family burdens to Himself and wanted her to know that He sees all. She didn't have to fix anyone or any situation. He wanted to move mightily in her family. Restoration and angels are all around her battle cry! He showed me a boat in the middle of the ocean. She was the one paying attention and crying out to God for help while everyone else was in chaos. Then He showed me a rope that was tied on to the bow, and it was a three cord strand as it stretched out into the ocean. Then I came upon His almighty hand as it grasped the strong cord. I saw the rope being pulled by His hands, one slowly overlapping the next. It was being led somewhere ... to the other side! I heard, "They will get to dry land and have all the victory and promises of God!" Whoa! This is so marvelous to witness for them. She was at her wit's end, but God reminded her that He is towing the rope! Be calm in the midst of the storm and He will bring you out better than before! Trust in what He is doing, and not what you see.

I just realized while I am writing this, how I had to go through each one of these lessons. Now He uses me for others. I had to go through all of these things myself in order to experience God. Skipping them would have been like having a seed and never seeing it sprout. I gasp at the idea of complete devastation. How ghastly it would be—to not see that stalk become a tall, full grown, mature man, who now bears the fruit.

I just heard, "We must invite God into our garden!" He comes to weed out and discard strangling roots. Prunes and chops. Cuts back and reveals to us truth which promotes our growth. Being freshly attended to gives us the excitement to share and speak into other's lives by the actualization of our experience. I am sure He could do this all on His own,

but He is choosing to use His disciple. I recall the yearning of my heart to be a vessel for the glory of God. I remember asking Him to hurry up and set me in my true destiny. I dreamed of the day I would arrive! Now I know I needed to not only go through these trials and tribulations, but I needed to gain the understanding to reveal it to others as He wants. I had thought I would help lost and hurting women in my path. Recently, He has brought perhaps seven or eight women in my pathway to give away His love to. This is a newly appointed position in Christ and a new awareness of working in the kingdom as a vessel for others. When God breathes on them through me, He has no obstacles to impede Him. He can blow through me to the other side to touch them. Wow!

This is total humility in its grandeur.

The scripture that he keeps bringing to the forefront in my mind is found in 2 Corinthians 10:17 and says, "However, let him who boast and glories boast and glory in the Lord."

There always seems to be a double lesson piggy-backing on the previous one! My neighbor tried to speak to me about diet and exercise in a healthy manner. Considering she and her husband are physical trainers with the Marines, you would think I would listen! Well, pride jumped in and the Lord had a talk with me as I grieved at my long-standing behavior. I asked Him, "Why do I do this, the things which I don't desire?" I was humbled as He revealed to me how I needed to listen more and be still!

The Still Small Voice

"Who, me?" I asked Him.

"Yes, you!" He answered.

What good is it if I am full, and letting other people know, if I am not hearing their heart and allowing God to speak to me through them? That would be totally selfish of me. I don't want to keep God just for myself. How can I adopt an environment where women want to talk about their deepest cares and pains if they didn't feel safe with me?

I didn't need to tell them what I know, but allow the Lord to minister to them. I needed more of God and less of my own voice! I experienced failure during the first two encounters, but craving for God's best, I humbled myself and let the Spirit flow. This has been an amazing transformation in me. It's not about what I know anymore, but what I can give away: the love of God and all His glory. Not mine, but His loving presence touching the lives of His children. As I write, a lump develops in my throat and tears are welling up as my heart softens with the awareness of how gentle His mercy is.

Submissively, I gladly turn into His likeness and then ask for more. Sanctified and set free from my selfish soul, brings me to a place of transformation by renewal and a willingness to obey His will. "More, Lord, More. I love you so. Amen"

I feel my life has taken a turn since September. It's as if I was just born. Something drastic changed. I can hardly remember what happened before that time, but I know my

eyes are ahead, looking forward with hope and promises. I am aware of the uncharted map that is placed before me. We are all somewhere unfamiliar. We can't continue doing what we know. I saw an obstacle course (vision) while listening to a young lady walking a crooked path. When you turn the corner, you don't know if there is a mud hole or if high hurdles are next. Perhaps a wall to climb, then a knee crawling path!

We were all so used to knowing the routine and what to expect declaring, "I got this, been there before." We were all self-sufficient and surely we didn't need God to show us anymore! Yikes! We took God out of the equation and added self. He has opened our eyes and we need to use them to see in the Spirit of God.

**He has moved us out of self-reliance
to become God-dependent.**

God has taken me out of the safe routine and set me into a place of transition. He wants to comfort and assure me today that it is He who is realigning me for His glory. I am so excited, to stand in encouraging praise in knowing how much the rewards are worth the price! He has loosed the remnants and sent them upon fertile ground—a place of re-seeding, plowing, and sowing in the next season.

It never feels good to be pruned, but today I have open arms to welcome the Great Groomer! It is exciting when the revelation comes that He is at the helm, and not me!

The Still Small Voice

"Lord, I welcome You to come and mess up my perfect garden! I trust You as I am constantly in Your loving arms of righteousness.

"What magnificent things You have done! Please see fit to use me in Your kingdom. You have used the big shears to cut off some very thick branches from me. Holy Spirit I welcome you. May your light shine in dark places as the enemy scatters. Free the chains off of Your little ones. Breathe on us. Make all things new as You say, 'Everyone is useable.' Please Lord, redesign our garden rows and plant new seed. Re-establish Your covenant with us and realign us with You. Amen."

Your child-like daughter,

Stephanie

The Still Small Voice

"Behold, I will do a new thing;
now it shall spring forth;
shall ye not know it?
I will even make a way
in the wilderness,
and rivers in the desert."

—Isaiah 43:19 KJV

Forty-Five

Beautiful

I awoke in the middle of the night last night and surprised the Holy Spirit! (Well, I really don't think He was surprised as much as I would like to think!) I saw me lying down, actually floating. I was in a white gown. Then I saw another of the same image floating above me. They were facing one another. It was later revealed to me, that it was my spirit communicating with another spirit! Spirit to spirit!

It was the Redemptive Spirit (I just heard)!

Awakening early in the morning, I had another experience! We had access to bring down heaven. Whoa! This was fresh revelation gifted to me. God revealed it to me as He wanted me to have it; I was given access at any time, to pull down heaven. Whatever is accessible, is available to me! It was released to me today. Many times I have seen a flower in the shape of a golden trumpet, opening to the heavens. It faces the heavens for feeding as the flower radiates from stretching upwards toward the sun. In this same way, our prayers have ability to bring heaven's glory down! This is truly a confirmation of a something that happened a few days ago at the post office. Gigantic angels appeared and changed the atmosphere from anger to ridiculous joy! I could see in the Spirit what was really happening in that realm! There was no warning time that said, "Hey, I'm gonna do something here and I need you to do it!" It just switched over and I was in the midst of it after He instructed me to declare peace as He notified me of the bitterness through out all the employees working there.

I was stunned and turned to my husband and said,"Look how angry everybody is." I verbally and boldly spoke into the atmosphere during our transaction with an angry man. Declaring peace out loud to him at the very tip of every deliberately offensive jab. I saw three enormous angels line up behind me, facing the counter. They were easily 30 feet tall! Stunningly, I saw the angels take over the place and everyone began to giggle! Even our clerk did a complete turnaround instantly and was overjoyed, laughing, and returned my blessing to him! I couldn't believe what I was seeing here! How exciting our God is!

I mark this as such a respectful, merciful, loving privilege to witness. I have learned there are many testings, and how we are to stand in a mighty position and watch God move when we pray and stand firm in Him. We are not to react to the situation in a worldly fashion. When we abide in Him continually, it's like we get to watch and participate, as our big Pappa moves in His imperial ways. It is so very exciting!

The Still Small Voice

"Lord, I am appreciative beyond words of the majestic glory of You and what heaven delivers to earth. Please qualify me in the kingdom-schooling. Be my teacher, counselor, friend, and Father. As I walk, teach me to run—to finish the race in victory!"

With a thankful heart and big smile,

Stephanie

The Still Small Voice

"I am my beloved's,
and his desire
is toward me."

—Song of Songs 7:10 NIV

Forty-Six

Overcomer

I thought last night was the end of the end ... until I turned completely to Him.

I realized in the midst of the battle field, I could not win this on my own. It was impossible. I tried to stay strong, but in my weakness, He brought me out victoriously!

I can't remember being this mad in a long time. Yes, I admit it fully. I spent countless hours preparing for my books to go to a publishing company. One goal I had set for December. The manuscripts were fragmented, misplaced, scrambled, filed incorrectly, plus more. How could this have happened? And to top it off, my accounting for our business vanished. Four months of work, disappeared from two days ago. Frustration didn't even come close to what I really felt.

I almost came to the point of relinquishing for peace sake and forgetting about any chance of submitting my writings and getting them published. But, up rose this spirit in me,

who knew how very important it was for me to finish this God-given agenda. It's as if this mighty wind just engulfed me with awesome power! New to me!

I am so thankful for my husband—not only for repairing my computer, but for making it better than before! He admittedly acknowledged that he didn't have a clue what to do. So we both know the knowledge came from God Himself through the favor of obedience from my husband. The Lord has given solutions for so many things that my husband has never attempted before. He has astonishing feats of victory! God has amazing ways of just downloading into him where, how, and why. I'm full of gratitude! If it were up to me, last night someone else would have had free ownership to this computer!

After spending two days of re-establishing the broken files, I finally realized that I was totally incapable of any further stress. I turned to God and He asked me what I wanted. I gave Him specifics and He showed me last night in a vision, how to file my writings. It looked very simple, yet in the computer it was a total disaster due to my lack of skills. I prayed for perfect peace in the storm. I sought to hide in Him from the enemy's plot. I had to really press in and turn away from the fleshly emotions.

So, I sat down, once again, and did what He said, and bingo! Perfect filing, simplified, complete, and just incredible. Believe me, this was all God-breathed and ordered into perfectness that surpassed all my understanding! I am not

The Still Small Voice

computer savvy to say the least! Beforehand, I placed my trust in Him, recalling the predicted results with God's hand, "Ya know, I will probably say after you miraculously fix this into perfection, 'This is working too easy, something's gotta be wrong, this is way too good!'"

"Not the confident believer," you say?

I had just given this same encouragement, "He is with you," to a friend this morning. In fact, I have given this to three people in the past few days! Now, I am in the battle recovery zone of my own words! Testing, testing, testing ... I think He was setting me up, but I overcame this past week!

I have learned that we cannot accomplish things in our own flesh. I knew this, but somehow slipped back into my old habits of self reliance! Evidently, I needed it to be duct taped to my own life!

Not only did my computer crash, but I could give you a whole laundry list of wrongs from the past five days. Speaking of laundry, I will share this one with you:

Have you ever filled a washer up with a full load of white clothes, then think your pouring laundry detergent over them? Only, too late, you come to realize you were pouring old dirty truck oil instead?

That's right! I poured truck oil from the last oil change all over my beautiful white clothes! It happened to be put in a pretty lavender-looking empty laundry container! Hmmm, I didn't see that one coming! I had to throw away all the

clothes. The good part ... and yes, there is a good part ... my favorite white shirt was spared! As I was loading the clothes, something inside me said, "Don't put it in the machine." It survived unscathed, not a drop of oil! In fact, all the items from that load were not a problem to toss out! Yep ... I now believe in Laundry Angels!

Oh, and did I mention the cell phone that dropped in the toilet? Good news ... we had the identical one as a spare! Even my favorite ringtone that I thought I lost, turned up after prayer this morning too! Of course, that was after the Cell Phone Angels arrived!

How about the passport? We needed it to arrive in our calendar time-frame, and were highly advised to spend excessive money for express delivery by an employee. To our delight, our overseer processed our passports with exponentially fast delivery—record time—and the best part is that we had only to pay regular postage price! Are you thinking what I'm thinking? Postal Angels too?

Then there was the Scooter that couldn't get registered because of wrongdoing from the dealership ... the lord took care of that too!

What the enemy meant for evil, He will always turn for my good. Always. My lesson comes from Joshua 1:8 in the Amplified:

> *"This book of the law shall not depart out of your mouth, but you shall meditate on it day and night, that you may observe and do*

The Still Small Voice

accordingly to all that is written in it. For then you shall make your way prosperous, and then you shall deal wisely and have good success."

It's just that He gave me this time to do specific things and I am so excited to do them. I want to walk them out to the completion line ... and do it in this lifetime. It is exciting to cross into the next thing, then the next! The enemy is trying to disturb, trap, and eat up my valuable time. But I know that I need to be in full submission and thankfulness as if it has already been done while on this assignment. More than ever. The giants are getting bigger, but so am I! The giants shall fall before me. Amen!

As I encounter reformation and circumcision, 1 Samuel 17 says:

So David prevailed over the Philistine with a sling and with a stone, and struck down the Philistine and slew him. But no sword was in David's hand.

In the midst of all the difficulties and obstacles, I am proud to say that last month I became a member of a local Art League! One which I never thought I was talented enough for. The Lord told me to begin this step to display my art. I know He will put the creations into action as I trust in Him only. I can't express enough how I see this coming together now. I foresee the plans He has for me that will bring a ministry of engagements through all this preparation. Trusting without seeing the goal line is a true testimony of faith. His voice will echo through the delivery of the finale of my book and our testimonies. Each will be a witness of

His great love. New talents, a by-product of our giftings, will certainly be the new curtain lifting upon the stage which He has prepared to show up.

So, if you think you are having a rough day or week, or longer, give yourself permission to move aside for the Father's breath. He takes center stage upon His arrival and bestows His abundant mercy and grace upon His children to lead them into green pastures. He is the great teacher and beholds the Father's desires. I can do nothing apart from Him. He makes me whole where the empty places are void. He establishes it all, into perfect harmony. It's time to put away self preservation and be totally dependant upon Him and watch how He renews me. I believe the future holds some mighty warriors of leadership to command His armies. (I just heard this.)

"Lord, You are my strength and my refuge, whom shall I fear? I love Your ways. Teach me all that You have for me. Enlighten my path. Make my ways perfect. I trust You. I believe You. Amen."

Your trooper and overcomer,

Stephanie

Forty-Seven

Jeremiah 29:11

What an exciting three months this has been! Our household had specific instructions and now I see the fruit. One was to study and focus on what He wanted us to do. God was clear that were were only to go where He said to go and do what He said to do.

The time was set aside for specific purposes and His agenda for us in our lives in order to regulate us and prepare us. We needed to have a more solid pattern in order to propagate His purpose in our lives. Specific times were given to me to exercise, to study, to write, to eat, to work, and even when to go to bed!

During this season my husband has officially become a United States citizen! This was an amazing season to bear witness of obeying and seeing the fruit grow! It had to be record time! Start to finish went so swiftly and was so effortless. I am so proud to see my husband rightfully

positioned for his future. I congratulate him and welcome him to the United States of America!

Through this change, the Lord convicted me to officially change my name to my married name. I had not done this yet due to my identity of self, selfishness, and the business. But now I cherish the process of aligning myself with my husband, so I am officially changing my name on all personal and business documents, I will be known as Mrs. Stephanie M. Lumbia! That's small, medium, and large! SML

This expedited us to a new place and we truly became one. My husband is overjoyed as I shower him with honor through this process. I can see clearly how much this meant to him. We both feel like we belong now: belong too one another and to Christ as one. It is the correct order of our Father. How overjoyed we are and my Father smiles!

The next step, stirred me to adapt the new change upon my passport and license. Do I hear traveling in the near future? Hmmm...

Since this all happened exponentially and swiftly, I asked the Lord, "Why?"

He answered. (... and like why should I even be surprised when He does answer, because He always does! He never returns it void!) He said, "This is ordering your steps."

It's preparation time for future endeavors. Procrastination is now cancelled on all levels of any hesitations! I am diligently seeking the Lord and having a relationship with

the One who made me, while being transformed through my obedience towards Him. He has not revealed the future of the "why's" and "wherefore's" and I'm not looking for them any longer. Instead I choose to trust by faith and stay in the light. After all Jeremiah 29:11 says:

> *"'For I know the plans I have for you,' declares the Lord, 'plans to prosper you and not to harm you, plans to give you hope and a future.'"*

"Lord, I trust in You being You! Amen."

Trusting,

Stephanie

The Still Small Voice

"... and the two shall become
one flesh. So they are
no longer two, but one."
—Mark 10:8 NIV

Forty-Eight

Provision

Our hunger could not be held back any longer. It was time for our spirit to get its feeding!

You know ... when you know ... when you know! And we knew we wanted desperately to go to our church to get fed!

The only setback ... our church is 233 miles away!

But, have no fear, for God is here! And where the Lord is, provision abides also!

When something inside of you calls to you, listen. Because it is not your instincts, but the Holy Spirit speaking through you, as one. There has been a shift in me about trusting the nudges, instincts, and subtle promptings that have been frequenting me. They are from the Holy Spirit dwelling in me. I was questioning if it was me or the Spirit. Now I know it is me and Him.

We are As One! Heeding the sound of His voice, however gentle, is God manifesting with one heart and mind inside me! This is truly a transformation that has taken some time for me to arrive at. It is a reward for complete sacrifice and obedience for craving nothing shorter than the completeness of an overturned life, in Christ. I can testify: where there is hunger, our Lord feeds!

As we headed back home, I pondered for a moment and as quickly as it came, it left as perfect Sabbath rest. I laid out in complete honesty to my Lord, while not uttering a word to my husband. "Lord, we are excited now to make this journey, but will it grow old after a time? We don't want it to lose its appeal because of distance. The long ride could become burdensome. It is a four hour trip just one way, and I believe we will be doing this on a more regular basis."

The moment I thought these words, I received this overwhelming, comforting peace, unlike before. "Let go and relax." Immediately I felt my shoulders fall and the burden fell off of me.

All false concerns left me. To this I was certain the Lord was present in our vehicle, because I looked up after my conversation with Jesus and saw Exit 8! Simultaneously, my husband and I turned to one another in astonishment! "It can't be!" It felt like we were in Charlotte, just ten minutes ago! How could this be? We just left there! Only two quick conversations, and we had already arrived home? "How was that possible? Am I dreaming?" I wondered.

With this amused bewilderment, a lighted gauge on our dashboard appeared that said, "Warning 3.0 hours." Never has that happened. We did not set any timer or mile gauge. It appears the truck even went through a time travel! The computer couldn't identify the reality of mileage vs. the time frame!

God miraculously took us 233 miles in ten minutes!

There was even more miraculous provision. We used only half of the gas consumption we normally use for this trip! We also received favor with the hotel for a lower rate, food, the same, shopping, even better! Upon our next return to church, I shared this with one of the members there and I'll never forget the look on her face! She told me we were, "Exponentially Transported!" I shook my head in agreement, but truthfully, I had no idea what that meant!

We had the honor to share a meal with a family in Christ while there. We even got to bless a women with a paid tab at the grocery store! He loves to share and give Himself to others. We love to participate with heaven. It's a win-win!

Seems like the message is, "If I send you there, I will make the provision to take you there and take care of all things."

"The Well of Plenty"

He watched over us and we even got a pat on the shoulder during worship from an usher. As I turned, we were asked to serve communion! My jaw just dropped open

in unexpected favor, as my husband finally moved from stunned, to "Absolutely, sir."

What an opportunity to serve and bless the children of God and to witness the impartation of God's love and honor to each person who partakes.

So, we came to get fed and He had us feed the body. This is an interesting way how the Father feeds us and we turn and give it away immediately.

I love when He does that!

> *"Blessed are those who hunger and thirst for righteousness, for they will be filled."*
> Matthew 5:6 NIV

"Lord, I bow before You and bask in the glorious light of Your presence. Thank You for **transporting** us from one place to another in an un-worldly explanation! Thank You for allowing us to share and boast of Your goodness, mercy, kindness, and loving care. How I love You so zealously!"

Provided for,

Stephanie M. Lumbia and *Leonardo Lumbia* !

Forty-Nine

Inheritance

An inheritance cannot be earned, worked for, or even begged for. It is given freely without hindrances, through the blood of the Divine One whom we call Jesus.

It is undeserving, and it's rightfully yours. You have been given it freely with only one way to receive it. It has been reserved for the righteous. Through the torturous death for all mankind, by the Pure One. To all, He is the plan to enter the kingdom's passageway. He is the path to freedom. He died to overcome the death of sinners. He came to fulfill the Gospel. He came to repel and break every sin of the world. He came to restore us to our rightful place at the right hand of the Father, upon the throne.

I am hearing: "Kings and priests of royalty shall shine upon the earth and rule with the mighty sword of life-giving waters. He shall feed your appetite and you shall drink from His well. Passion will rule your heart and wisdom shall be your guide. With pillars and towers of strength shall you

overcome. The Lord's hand shall be your way and you shall reign ... yes, the remnants—the chosen ones.

"Dwell in thy tents and stretch as far as the east is to the west. Take up thy holiness of heaven and carry the Word with dignity and power. Endorse the everlasting with vigor and zeal. With power on high and overwhelming victory shall He stand and rejoice, for this is the kingdom of God and He shall rule thy place. It has been established in heaven first and now arises across this nation in due timing of the great I Am."

"Lord, arise in me! With all that You are in me, arise! Leave nothing uncovered or unused. Use me for Your glory. For I belong to You because You first loved me. I receive all the inheritance stored up for me. I receive Jesus Christ as my personal Savior and Lord and repent for my sins. I give You my life. Amen."

I receive the abundant life!

Stephanie

Fifty

The Wilderness

An interesting thing happened today. The Lord had me text a friend (and then some) regarding our whereabouts!

I sent her this: "A beautiful place my husband and I are at! It's 'The wilderness!' It's where He chose to place us, where we can be just with Him. There is total fullness there. He is teaching us to be ready for things that will come next! It's a great place to go to. This is the second time He has placed me here. We are going to come out in an awesome way. Ready to do what he wants. It's our church, the awesome school of the Holy Spirit!"

He was preparing me for what is to come and it's going to be grand. Actually humongous! I know next year is overflowing with multitudes of "Power" in the house of the Lord. It will be unlike any other year!

January will kick off with eye openers and opportunities to step into. He will move us into position, geographically to receive from others. My Father has revealed His authority and power to be used through us. I am so excited! I know

I can't do this alone and it is only going to manifest by my complete dependency on Him. But I anticipate such a wonderful and magnificent explosion from the Lord. This is the year for us!

All my transformation of body, heart, and mind are now going to be placed into the future for His use. The inadequacies of the human downfall will be uplifted by the grace of God and His all enduring purpose—His intention to reconcile Himself unto mankind in all His glory.

I recognize now that I have been taken out of the ordinary and put into the extraordinary! I have been swept away for four months now, just bathing in His wisdom and love for me. He has accelerated my growth into a more mature, obedient, and worthy servant of the Lord. I am a committed, loyal servant who hangs on every word that proceeds out of the mouth of the Lord Jesus Christ. Truly!

The wilderness is where I am just smothered in His presence. It is where He lathers me with riches and bathes me in oil. He stretches me to inherit His good favor. He enlarges my tent and grants me permission to grow and tangle with Him like a grapevine, intertwining me into His secret chamber. He speaks to me ever so gently in so many different ways. He stirs me to ask Him questions, and not be silent. We have communion, a true relationship embellished by His divine nature: who He really is.

Interestingly, He revealed to me why the heels of both my feet were in dire pain in the last wilderness adventure. In the natural, I thought it was my shoes, from work, or from playing tennis. But in the Spirit, it was victory! I was bruising the head of Satan!

I weep at the thought, "I never knew you." For some will miss out who He really is. To conquer the depths of such a Man who is so madly in love with us. He is for us and rooting in our corner all the time. He desires to help us, but do we ask? The value He puts on us, the world could not put a price on. Yet we seek Him not?

I hear Him saying, "For the answers are not within your reach because you have not asked your Helper. For I cannot accomplish all I have called you to by your fleshly thinking."

When I breathe Him in, we exhale together. It's like one constant motion. He goes everywhere I go. He even speaks for me at times. He sets up my day and moments without me missing a beat. When His glory moment comes, I cry. I weep with such endearing love for Him that He comforts me and delights in my acknowledgement of what He just did. I sink into this place of sweet humbleness, filled in the extravagant love I see. There are times, when I am public, and tears just roll down my face, unstoppable because of His vast love for me and how incredibly beautiful He is.

Yes, we're in the wilderness. It's a place of being doted on by God. It's a place that I love to go to now. It's safe and warm. It's truly a place of grace. I know I will have to come out to this old world. I am like a cocoon, wrapped in His arms. It is a place of justice, to all who enter. It is like having a joyful chat over a cup of tea, but the tea never runs out!

I'm in a new place with Him. I am experiencing His overflowing love. I feel His arms around me and His heart is too big to speak of! How I embrace His house, the place above the mantle. The house with the big doors and the big chair. The playfulness of delighted hearts. It is a place where you can be your childlike self and He delights in His creation of you. It is the place where heaven rejoices with the jubilee of colorfulness, sunshine, and music. There are colorful fields of flowers and domes for homes. It is a place of perfect harmony and a community of unity. All together as one family under God.

"Your joy makes my joy!"

"Lord, thank You for embracing me patiently with such power of enduring. I love you dearly and all that you created me to be. I am Your daughter, whom You knew before time."

Cradled in grace,

Stephanie

Fifty-One

Be Prepared

As we traveled westward, away for the celebration for the coming year, I wanted to write about the words spoken to me by my Father:

"Be prepared! Next year is going to be so powerful! He will have strategic placement for His Saints and then the power of Christ is going to rise. He Reigns!"

We celebrated the ending of last year and the beginning of this next season at church with vibrant movements! It was the best season ever! I had an overwhelming amount of peace and such joy ... not possible from the worldly holiday! We are not under anyone's law or restricted to our works any longer! It has been a time set apart for refreshment in His holy rejuvenating system! And where there is rest, there is perfect peace and love. This is divine happiness!

As we began worshipping, His Spirit emerged. "Catch on fire," I heard, and interpretation of tongues, "I'm fixed here,"

He said. It was certain His presence abided here through the thick anointing engulfing the entire atmosphere!

I saw a magnificent race horse in a full throttle run. His gallant breathtaking mane was curled into a dominant spiral fashion, in breathtaking hues of green. Interestingly, the horse had reigns on. I believe this is a "Warrior Horse." Something new I have never seen before! This season is the coming of the new. He is directing the path of the Warrior Horse with the reigns. He comes rushing in and His mighty wind will follow as it passes by. It is coming with majestic, unmistakable power, and He will reign! Get ready! For it is the forthcoming of the almighty King Himself who will reign and rule in an overturned government exchange of power!

I stand upon His promises for me will come in this fresh New Year. The storehouse gates will be released! I heard, "growth of generations ..." when we prayed over finances!

I am so excited for the New Year. I anticipate Godly wisdom, supernatural healings, miracles, angels, atmospheres, riches, power, and surmountable changes. He will reign! He will take territory. He showed me the world from outside the universe. It was Him looking upon the earth. At that very moment, He brought up the verse about even the cattle on the hillside are His. Then the true revelation came ... He owns everything! I know I have heard this before and agreed with it, but tonight, the impact engulfed me in conviction. The world is all His and everything in it! He has ownership of all. He created the universe and the people, and it all came with a price tag of … "You are Mine!"

Nothing is ours, for we are mere caretakers of His abundant gifts. I wonder how many other people really have this notion. We seem to strive for the good life and cherish proudly what we own and possess. In actuality, it's not yours to keep. But we think we are entitled to prosperity by our works. We accumulate worldly things and put a value on them. How they comfort us when we are surrounded by them! Yikes! Have you ever measured up to a household of pretty coordinated tableware, that endorse your identity in Christ? Does a diamond ring comfort you the way your heavenly Father embraces you and lets you know how pleasing you are to Him, just as you are?

Reality and truth are imperative to have. It's not yours, so stop holding on to things and their tangible efforts to measure your position on earth. Your success isn't measured in this capacity by your Father. And I'm not just talking about material things. This also encompasses past hurts, infirmity, ideas, thoughts, as well as self-righteous beliefs about God. We should know better, but none-the-less, we still haven't got it correctly yet. All these things will fade away. They have more than once for me and my household!

Perhaps this is a message for me to lighten up the load. Rid myself of the backpack. I am to dispose of the unuseable stuff in the kingdom, harboring things I think we might need later. I hold on to the belongings which catch only dust. I

need to let go of the possessions I hold so dearly, but are hindering me. Not only the visible ones, but also the invisible ones. I need to be mobile and ready for when He calls me out. I need to be free from laboring, striving, and trusting my own understanding. The true and only thing I have need of is the Father's love and presence.

When we turn from the "items" and fill up on Him, everything else becomes dim. "So," I ask, "How dim is your light and how bright is His?"

That certainly is something to soak in for a minute or two! Whose light shines when you face the world daily? How much are you willing to lay down? How much does He really mean to you in your life? At what cost are you prepared to truly follow the cross. Selflessly or selfishly? Whose eyes do you see through every day? What's your heart say? Do you have ears to hear? Do you have His thoughts or other thoughts? Are you a true vessel living in the Holy Spirit?

There is no condemnation in Christ, only true life. "Freedom" like I have never experienced to this extent. I have stepped away from self the past four months and received the freedom to be with God in my life. It's where you bare yourself to Him, permitting you to be visible to the core. And then like an ocean of rushing water, being cleansed through the refreshing water we call blood. He pours into me and fills me to overflowing, automatically causing me to release it and give it away, as He plans. He is so ever gentle in all He does. For He lives in me and I am His forever. Nothing can clutch me out of His palm!

His inheritance word He gave me is, "Everlasting." He is going to stay, He is fixed, and He is generational. All things are new in me. Freedom reigns and I will inherit the promises ... and I am, on fire for Him!

Praising and thanksgiving brings the anointing and the anointing breaks all the yolks.

"Lord, I lay my flesh down entirely. Restore me to the foundation of truth. Place me at the point of rebirth You began. Rewind and recoil my youthful days of childhood. Reset and renew me, then teach me Thy ways. I will listen and I will grow into all truth and into righteous pathways. Bring me to a place of obedience with care. I will uphold the fragility of mercy bestowed upon my head. Build the tabernacle You once began. Mark me as, "Returned to Sender," my heavenly Father. Reposition me into righteousness," I pray.

"The coming of the New Year is going to mark a year of favor. Embellish me Lord. Quicken me to Your likeness. Use me to carry out Your will. Train me, stretch me, and position me for greatness. I trust You in the areas that have not yet fully developed. I ask that You ready me exponentially as we go. I promise to depend on You, who is in me, and I in You. For You are all sufficient for all I am called to do. I go willingly and wholeheartedly. I will sacrifice everything that

The Still Small Voice

You ask me to. I will rejoice with gladness and boast of your goodness, mercy, and love."

Prepared,

Stephanie

Fifty-Two

It's in the Small Things

I was given more insight on a revelation I had yesterday! Oh, the Lord cradles me in joy and love. He holds me in His arms with His breath over me. I have chills all over just at the vision of what this looks like!

His endearing heart of love was imparted to me. I caught a glimpse of what He has in store for me. I want to just stay here with Him as I write ... and I think, I shall!

Before our ministry class last night, my husband ran into the pharmacy for some mints. I waited in our vehicle outside of the shopping center. I glanced out the front window, and my head was drawn toward the right, where a gift card store was. The Lord took me on a journey!

I saw a small cart outside filled with merchandise. A thought ran past me. If left unattended, someone could steal something from it! And then I actually saw the cart left unaccompanied overnight. I was shown a woman standing inside the store and knew her thoughts about that. To her,

they were insignificant small gifts. If stolen, not to worry, because they didn't hold much value to her.

The next picture took me back to when I owned a boutique and I saw a child's dress that had a ruffled toile skirting and was pink. (Which, by the way, I never had anything like that in my shop!) So, I see this pretty, feminine dress as it passes toward the register counter. I had always delighted in giving away a small gift with the children's purchases. They were cubic Zirconia earrings that stood up on a cardboard display at the checkout counter. I could have easily sold them, but I gave them away instead. The objective of giving them away at no cost seemed to be highlighted to me. Bringing this thought captive, it prompted me to ask, "Why Lord? Why didn't I charge for them like other retail shops would?"

He answered, "Because you like to give things away. You would give it all away for free!"

My hands opened with my palms up, and my arms made a gesture of giving freely as they fanned open.

My heart leaped forward, as this was the total truth!

"I would give it all away for free"

By this moment, I was sitting in class with tears in my eyes because of the true understanding of what my Father had just revealed. I can't stop them from flowing as this locks into my heart. I am wrecked beyond measure.

As He continued to give me more revelation, it became clear to me that the Lord knew what was really in my heart.

The Still Small Voice

Money was not the center, but the endearing joy of giving gifts freely, was my foundation of truth. The woman in my vision didn't see the value in the small things, but when I gave those small earrings, it wasn't small to me. It meant a whole lot more because it came from my heart. They represented genuine diamonds!

It wasn't insignificant, it was immense, and I gave it in that manner!

The Lord will use me for even the smallest things as the world sees them, because I give them with the grandeur of Him. I naturally honored strangers with free gifts. For it is His reflection and His heart that goes out to them. They get to visit with Jesus! And to Jesus, this means everything!

I hear in my spirit, *"It's not small to Me. It's all valuable beyond measure."*

Lord, all of the treasures of You are immense in the measure of their size. Do with me as you please, I am Yours.

"Open out your hands and give it away, for I am with you," I hear in my spirit.

Lord, I love sharing Your love and who You are. Use me beyond measure. Amen.

I hold all of your hidden treasures as precious,

Stephanie

The Still Small Voice

"If you are faithful in the small things, you will also be faithful in the large ones."

—Luke 16:10 NLT